44 ENGLAND'S NUMBER 1
Bob Wilson on Seaman, James, Martyn, Wright and Co.

46 STORY OF THE SEASON Part IV: THE FA CUP
How Wycombe Wanderers rekindled that old cup magic and Liverpool scooped the ultimate prize.

50 ENGLAND EXPECTS!
Insider pics of England stars in training.

52 CAN ANYONE STOP MANCHESTER UNITED?
Will the Red Machine steamroller to a fourth title in a row?

54 STYLE FILE #2: SUIT YOU, SIR!
Glam football stars in glam gear… Eat your heart out, Barry Venison!

55 MAGIC MOMENTS No.3
Andy Townsend picks his top incident of 2000/01.

56 STAT ATTACK!
The best passers, the top scorers and the biggest foulers… all the Premiership stats are right here.

58 THE BIG ONE: WORLD CUP 2002
What can we expect when Japan and South Korea host the biggest football show on earth.

60 MAGIC MOMENTS No.4
Housewives' favourite Des Lynam selects his top action from last season.

62 QUIZ #2: GO GLOBAL!
Test your knowledge of world football with our globe-trotting international quiz.

63 PREMIERSHIP SUPERSTARS: DAVID BECKHAM

ITV SPORT PREMIERSHIP ANNUAL 2002

Editorial: Aubrey Ganguly & Justyn Barnes
Art Director: Oliver Smee
Designer: Ceri Thomas
Cartoons: Tony Husband
Photographs: Action Images
ITV behind-the-scenes photos: Shona Wong
Statistics:  opta.co.uk

Thanks to: Derek Balment, Martin Corteel, Chris Hawkes, James Pinniger, Paul Tyrrell and all the team at *On The Ball*.

THIS IS A CARLTON BOOK
This edition published in 2001 by
Carlton Books Limited
20 Mortimer Street
London W1T 3JW

10 9 8 7 6 5 4 3 2 1

Text and design copyright © 2001, Carlton Books Limited

A CIP catalogue record for this book is available from the British Library

ISBN 1 84222 406 9

Printed and bound in Italy

Contents 03

WELCOME

Every year, Premiership football throws up new characters, new stories and new drama. And this season, we're going to be there every step of the way, giving you expert opinion and top coverage as all the excitement unfolds...

Terry Venables

Gabby Yorath

Ally McCoist

Barry Venison

Andy Townsend

Clive Tyldesley

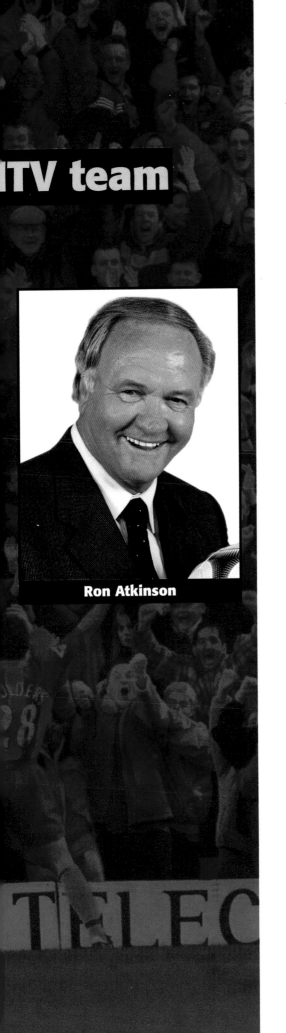

Ron Atkinson

Hello and welcome to the *ITV Sport Premiership Annual 2002*! We're delighted to have Premiership football action back on ITV and are looking forward to a great season. Manchester United have dominated over the past couple of years, but it looks like the title race will be a lot tighter this time. Of course, Sir Alex Ferguson will be determined to win a fourth title in a row in his final season as manager at Old Trafford and new signings such as the £19 million man Ruud Van Nistelrooy will only help his quest. But United's old rivals Liverpool are finally showing signs of a true revival – Gerard Houllier's men performed extraordinarily well in cup competitions in 2000/01 and now it's a question of whether they can translate that form into league consistency. Meanwhile, Leeds United, Arsenal and Chelsea will be desperate to fulfil their potential and mount a sustained challenge for the title. It will also be interesting to see how Ipswich Town follow up their fairytale return to the Premiership and whether Jean Tigana's Fulham side can emulate the Tractor Boys in their first season back in the top flight. All in all, the 2001/02 Premiership promises to be a cracker, just like this ITV annual. Packed full of star features, facts and figures and football fun, it's bound to whet your appetite for another thrilling year of football action from the most exciting league in the world. Enjoy!

Des

STRIKING TALENT

England is blessed with a batch of excellent strikers. Andy Cole, Robbie Fowler, Emile Heskey, Michael Owen and Kevin Phillips have all been banging in goals, but who will win Sven-Goran Eriksson's vote at international level. Let's check the form of the fab five...

ANDY COLE

Despite his superb goalscoring record for Manchester United, Andy Cole is still decried by his critics for missing too many chances. They say he only scores so many goals for United because of the brilliant service he receives from David Beckham and co. But statistics do not support that view. Andy's average goals-to-shots ratio of 25% over the past three league seasons is superior to United colleagues Teddy Sheringham and Ole Gunnar Solskjaer and equalled only by Dwight Yorke. Furthermore, Andy's status as United's all-time top European Cup goalscorer of all-time with a total of 18 goals shows he has the class to perform at the top level. And the fact that Cole has been Sir Alex Ferguson's first-choice striker for the past six years speaks volumes.

Previous England managers such as Terry Venables and Glenn Hoddle were unconvinced though and his international chances have been very limited. But new boss Sven-Goran Eriksson has warmed to Andy's superb all-round game. Indeed, when the media and England fans were clamouring for Cole to be dropped after missing one easy chance against Finland, Sven stuck by his man. Andy repaid that faith by scoring his first international goal in the next game against Albania. Let's hope it's the start of a goal rush.

COLE TRIVIA
- He's got record decks at home and likes to do a bit of DJing at the weekend.
- Andy has a young son called Devante.
- He once released a record called 'Outstanding'... but it wasn't!
- Andy was voted the PFA Young Player Of The Year in 1994.
- He has his own charity which raises money for homeless kids in Africa.

BIG RON'S VIEW
"Coley has developed his all-round game so much over the last few years with Manchester United. Now, he's got off the mark, he might start banging them in regularly for England too."

ROBBIE FOWLER

Probably the most natural finisher in England, Robbie Fowler's meteoric career was held back by injuries in recent years. But he stormed back to prominence in 2000/01 helping Liverpool to a cup treble. 16 goals in 47 appearances suggest he is not as prolific as he once was, but he now has a more rounded game and retains the happy knack of scoring important goals.

Robbie scored six of his season total in the Worthington Cup including a hat-trick in the record 8–0 victory at Stoke in the fourth round and one of five Liverpool goals in the semi-final second-leg win over Crystal Palace at Anfield. He saved the best for the final at the Millennium Stadium though scoring with a brilliant instinctive strike and also drilling home a penalty in Liverpool's dramatic shoot-out win.

Because of the severe competition for places in Liverpool's team, Robbie occasionally has to sit it out on the bench, but if he stays injury-free, don't bet against him spearheading England's attack in World Cup 2002. He certainly has all the natural ability to do so.

FOWLER TRIVIA
- He scored on his League debut for Liverpool against Fulham and bagged five more goals in the return match!
- Robbie has two kids and says fatherhood has made him 'a bit calmer'!
- In the 1994/95 season, he scored a hat-trick against Arsenal in 4 minutes 32 seconds.
- Robbie was Liverpool's top scorer for four seasons in a row from 1993 to 1996.
- Robbie wears a special nose patch during games to help his breathing.

BIG RON'S VIEW
"A natural born finisher. Fowler has a sensational left foot and, on his day, he's a goalkeeper's worst nightmare. Last season, he showed signs of getting back to his best."

EMILE HESKEY

Muscular Emile became Liverpool's most expensive player when he joined the club from Leicester City for £11 million in March 2000. A good team player with the ability to hold the ball up, the only question mark against Heskey after he'd first few months at Liverpool was whether he'd score enough goals. His unselfish tendency to drift into wide positions and provide crosses for others was all very well, but Gerard Houllier wanted his powerhouse striker to use his physique and aerial ability to do more damage in the opposition penalty box. Emile proved he was a quick learner and scored goals for fun in 2000/01 ending up with an excellent goal tally of 22 goals in 55 games.

"The manager keeps drumming into me how good I am and I'm finally starting to believe it," said happy Emile.

A former England Under-18 and Under-21 international, Emile is now a fixture in the England squad. So far Sven-Goran Eriksson has mainly employed him as a substitute to bring on as a winger and terrorise tired full backs. But if he keeps improving at the current rate, 23-year old Heskey could be England's main man by World Cup 2002.

HESKEY TRIVIA
- Garage music fan Emile is good mates with DJ Spoony from the Dreem Teem.
- Emile once played alongside Michael Owen in the England Under-18 team.
- He won two Worthington Cup winners' medals with Leicester City.
- He scored three goals during Liverpool's triumphant 2000/01 UEFA Cup campaign.
- Emile won a penalty just three minutes into his Liverpool debut against Sunderland.

MICHAEL OWEN

Michael Owen has had to carry a huge weight of expectation since his wonder goal against Argentina in the 1998 World Cup finals. But he clearly has the talent and attitude to be an England player for the next decade.

In the past couple of years, he has been troubled by hamstring problems. It's not an unusual problem for players who possess electric pace – Manchester United winger Ryan Giggs has had similar difficulties. When he is injury-free though, Owen is without doubt one of the most exciting players in world football.

Last season, Michael banged in 24 goals in 45 games for Liverpool and there were some memorable strikes among them. No Liverpool fan will ever forget his two match-winning goals against Italian league leaders Roma in the UEFA Cup fourth round away leg. And his two-goal salvo in the 2001 FA Cup final broke Arsenal fans' hearts while underlining his ability to score vital goals from half-chances.

Now he has just got to convince Sven-Goran Eriksson that he has the all-round game to justify a regular place in his England XI.

OWEN TRIVIA
- Michael was voted the 1998 BBC Sports Personality Of The Year.
- He made his England debut aged just 18 to become the youngest player to play for England in the 20th century.
- He has a crisp flavour named after him – 'Cheese and Owen'!
- Mike's childhood hero was Gary Lineker.
- Michael supported Everton as a kid!

KEVIN PHILLIPS

For someone who was advised to play at full back in his youth, Kevin Phillips makes a pretty good striker. A late starter, Watford manager Glenn Roeder gave him his first real chance in league football paying Dr Martens Southern League team Baldock Town a measly £10,000 for his services in 1994. His goal-every-two-games record for Watford attracted the attention of Sunderland boss Peter Reid who snapped up Kev for £325,000 in 1997. It was a sound investment. Kev scored 35 goals in his first season with the Black Cats, breaking Brian Clough's post-war club goalscoring record and forming a lethal partnership with lanky Niall Quinn.

Even though he missed three months of 1998/99 with a broken toe, Kev still mustered 25 goals to help Sunderland to the First Division Championship and earn his first England cap against Hungary in April 1999.

People wondered how he'd cope playing in the Premiership but Kevin gave the perfect reply scoring 30 goals in his first year in the top flight. Unfortunately, he didn't quite maintain that form in 2000/01 and he will now be looking to re-assert his England credentials.

PHILLIPS TRIVIA
- Kev once worked in a bakery to supplement his £200-a-week earnings at Baldock Town.
- As a trainee at Southampton, Kevin cleaned Alan Shearer's boots.
- Southampton youth coaches told Kev he was too short to be a striker!
- Kev rates "a fit Robbie Fowler" as the best striker in England.
- Kevin thinks apprentices should do work experience in a factory "so they can see what it's like in the real world".

BIG RON'S VIEW
"Niggling hamstring injuries affected him early on in 2000/01, but his late-season form, especially that FA Cup-winning performance against Arsenal, was magnificent."

BIG RON'S VIEW
"Phillips didn't play to his full potential in 2000/01 and he'll be looking to catch Sven's eye this year. He's got the talent to play for England, but faces stiff competition."

BIG RON'S VIEW
"Heskey has improved his game a lot since he joined Liverpool. He's shown he can score goals regularly for a top club and he is also a useful wing option for Sven."

HOW THEY MATCH UP *Premiership statistics 2000/01*

PLAYER	COLE	FOWLER	HESKEY	OWEN	PHILLIPS
Goals	9	8	14	16	14
Shots On Target	17	25	43	42	52
Shots Off Target	26	26	39	28	60
Blocked Shots	7	11	30	12	16
Goals-to-shots Ratio	21%	16%	17%	23%	13%

PEOPLE SAY THE FUNNIEST THINGS...

"Too many players are spending too much time playing golf and using the internet."

Dick Advocaat has a dig at his players' hobbies.

"It's like all beautiful things. It brings you problems but you can't resist the attraction."

Terry Venables on the FA Cup.

"I got sick of watching Richard and Judy."

Steve Bruce describes his time away from football management.

"Life isn't fair. If it was, it would be called fair. But it's not, it's called life."

Tony Adams explains the, er, meaning of life.

"The baby is being breast-fed at the moment. I'm leaving that to her mum because I don't think my chest is big enough!"

Robbie Fowler on the joys of parenthood.

"They have a few drinks and some prawn sandwiches but they don't know what's going on out on the pitch."

Roy Keane's dig at some Manchester United fans.

"It's made fish more important, so everyone's buying more."

Dennis Bergkamp explains how his in-laws, who are fishmongers, benefitted from foot and mouth.

"The professor told me I am clinically cured. I'm alright."

Ronaldo's way of saying he's fit again.

"I think I'll buy a crane and get one of those steel balls to start smashing on the manager's door."

Steve Guppy's threat to get manager Peter Taylor's attention.

"You wouldn't want to be in a bleeding war with them, would you?"

Harry Redknapp questions the backbone of tabloid journalists who are always changing their mind.

"I didn't do anything – other than help a few people over the wall. It was just a bit of fun."

Les Ferdinand confesses his part in the destruction of the Blue Peter garden.

"If I'm not doing my job properly, I get sacked. If a player isn't doing his job properly, he gets dropped. And referees? I don't know what happens to them..."

Peter Reid questions the men in black.

"My dream is to be second-best. Only then will I worry about those freaks from across the Pennines."

David O'Leary claims Manchester United are uncatchable… for the moment.

"When I finish my work, I don't watch football. I prefer other things."

Gabriel Batistuta reckons he's not a football fan.

"I was told that Stan was jetting out to New York to try and find his way into the movies."

Southend boss Dave Webb reveals details of Stan Collymore's last transfer.

THE PREMIERSHIP

AUGUST

The dawn of a new Premiership season is a time for big signings and a time to dream of glory. Big signings? Well, supporters of newly-promoted Manchester City are buzzing after acquiring the services of George Weah, the former World Footballer of the Year, from Chelsea. Meanwhile, Aston Villa fans hope David Ginola can add flair to John Gregory's workmanlike side.

Dreams of glory? Unfancied Coventry (minus Robbie Keane, who joins Internazionale for £13 million) and Newcastle both make promising starts, winning two of their first three games to finish August in fourth and third respectively.

The mood at table-toppers Arsenal is less optimistic though. Midfielder Patrick Vieira is considering his future in English football after being harshly sent-off twice in Arsenal's opening two games. Gunners' boss Arsene Wenger accuses opponents of deliberately trying to "upset Patrick" and then dismisses his club's chances of winning the league title saying they simply can't compete with Manchester United.

United's early-season form doesn't justify Wenger's pessimism though, as they struggle to away draws at Portman Road and Upton Park. George Burley's Ipswich side put up a particularly impressive performance against the Reds. Young Titus Bramble sets the tone in the opening

minutes with a thumping tackle on United hard man Roy Keane and the East Anglian club gain a deserved 1–1 draw.

On a sad note, news breaks of the death of Blackburn Rovers' chairman Jack Walker, whose millions helped Rovers to pip Manchester United for the Premiership title back in 1994/95.

SEPTEMBER

Despite starting the month at the bottom of the table, West Ham manager Harry Redknapp doesn't seem too bothered. "At least I can still get petrol," he says, as the rest of the country struggles in the fuel crisis.

It's definitely not a good month for Chelsea fans. Blues boss Gianluca Vialli is a surprise departure from the Premiership. The shock sacking of the popular Italian takes everyone by surprise. The players certainly don't seem to react well. There are defeats at the hands of Leicester City (which sees Hasslebaink and Panucci involved in an on-pitch bust-up) and St Gallen in the UEFA Cup as the club look for a new coach. Head of their list is Spaniard Jose Antonio Camacho, but eventually it is the former Valencia coach Claudio Ranieri who takes over the reigns at Stamford Bridge.

The club still seem in some confusion. There are rumours that Dennis Wise is the Chelsea board's main consultant on the appointment. Meanwhile, his team-mates make public their

opinions that it wasn't anything to do with a player revolt. Nonetheless, Frank Lebeouf is openly booed during the 1–0 win over St Gallen and Gianfranco Zola announces he has "a clear conscience". And the fans still chant Vialli's name.

Aston Villa's Luc Nilis ponders a career away from football after a career-threatening leg break following a clash with Ipswich's Richard Wright while Manchester United's Andy Cole gets picked as the lone striker for England's friendly against France.

Despite coming in for some criticism from the press, Kevin Keegan is vindicated by a fluent performance from his team as they manage an impressive away draw with the World and European champions.

Of bigger significance to the Premiership, however, is the possibility of transfer fees being scrapped following a directive from the European Union. A worldwide panic is threatened by clubs' fears that multi-million pound signings could walk away on freebies.

THE TOP...

Team	Pld	W	D	L	F	A	GD	Pts
1 Arsenal	3	2	0	1	7	4	+3	6
2 Leeds United	2	2	0	0	4	1	+3	6
3 Newcastle United	3	2	0	1	5	4	+1	6

THE BOTTOM...

Team	Pld	W	D	L	F	A	GD	Pts
18 Derby County	3	0	2	1	6	7	-1	2
19 Southhampton	3	0	2	1	6	7	-1	2
20 West Ham United	3	0	1	2	4	7	-3	1

PLAYER OF THE MONTH

Matt Clarke, Goalkeeper, Bradford City

Mins on pitch	270
Goals	
Goals conceded	1
Clean sheets	2
Saves	
Inside box	16
Outside box	8
Saves-to-shots ratio	96%

FORM TEAM

Newcastle United

v Manchester United (a)	lost 0–2
v Derby County (h)	won 3–2
v Tottenham Hotspur (h)	won 2–0

THE TOP...

Team	Pld	W	D	L	F	A	GD	Pts
1 Manchester United	7	4	3	0	20	7	+13	15
2 Leicester City	7	4	3	0	7	2	+5	15
3 Newcastle United	8	4	1	3	8	7	+1	13

THE BOTTOM...

Team	Pld	W	D	L	F	A	GD	Pts
18 Chelsea	7	1	4	2	10	12	-2	7
19 Bradford City	8	1	3	4	4	12	-8	6
20 Derby County	8	0	5	3	14	19	-5	5

PLAYER OF THE MONTH

Michael Owen, Striker, Liverpool

Mins on pitch	267
Goal Attempts	
Goals	5
Shots on target	8
Shots off target	1
Blocked shots	1
Goals-to-shot ratio	50%

FORM TEAM

Leicester City

v Ipswich Town (h)	won 2–1
v Southampton (h)	won 1–0
v Chelsea (a)	won 2–0
v Everton (h)	drew 1–1

OCTOBER

Arsene Wenger is hit with a 12-match touchline ban and a £100,000 fine following the tunnel bust up with a fourth official immediately after their game against Sunderland. The Arsenal manager's response is to threaten to sue the FA.

The FA have problems of their own, namely trying to find a successor to Kevin Keegan, after the England manager's decision to quit. Among the Premiership names being linked with the job are Charlton's Alan Curbishley and Leicester's Peter Taylor. Some of the media want to see Terry Venables back in the role.

Sven-Goran Eriksson is eventually announced as national coach although the appointment isn't to take place until the end of the season. As a stop-gap, Howard Wilkinson is employed to lead the national side to a 0-0 draw in Finland.

Fulham continue to knock on the Premiership's door as they equal the record for consecutive victories after winning their first 11 games of the season in the Nationwide First Division. Meanwhile, Peter Taylor's Leicester side are top of the Premiership.

At the other end of the table, Manchester City are struggling and George Weah departs the club for Marseille.

One thing to cheer up Arsene Wenger is the form of Thierry Henry whose run of goals include a superb strike against Manchester United in a hard-earned 1-0 victory at Highbury. Chelsea also get themselves back on track with a 3-0 win over Liverpool and a 6-1 thrashing against Coventry City.

NOVEMBER

Bryan Robson appears to be struggling at the Riverside and Terry Venables is rumoured to be on his way to Middlesbrough. Also struggling is Tottenham's George Graham after Spurs crash out to Birmingham in the Worthington Cup. Tottenham fans respond by calling for Alan Sugar's resignation.

The appointment of Eriksson continues to dominate the newspapers with PFA chief executive, Gordon Taylor claiming: "I think it will all end in tears. I can't see it working out."

Leicester City's excellent start begin to waver while manager Peter Taylor has to prepare for England's visit to Italy for another international friendly. He makes his mark on the squad however by picking a number of the Premiership's younger stars. Most notably, he makes David Beckham captain. Despite losing 1-0, England put up a spirited performance. The papers urge the FA to forget Sven and keep Taylor in charge instead.

At Chelsea, manager Ranieri starts to wave the chequebook and signs Jesper Gronkjaer from Ajax for £7.6m.

Manchester City are still struggling although confidence is high. Nicky Weaver claims: "The first thing Manchester City have to do is stay up, which I think we will do comfortably."

THE TOP...

Team	Pld	W	D	L	F	A	GD	Pts
1 Manchester United	11	7	3	1	31	8	+23	24
2 Arsenal	11	7	3	1	22	10	+12	24
3 Liverpool	11	6	3	2	20	14	+6	21

THE BOTTOM...

Team	Pld	W	D	L	F	A	GD	Pts
18 Southampton	11	2	4	5	12	20	-8	10
19 Bradford City	11	1	4	6	5	17	-12	7
20 Derby County	11	0	5	6	16	28	-12	5

PLAYER OF THE MONTH

Emile Heskey, Striker, Liverpool

Mins on pitch	360

Goal Attempts

Goals	5
Shots on target	11
Shots off target	3
Blocked shots	1
Goals-to-shots ratio	33%

FORM TEAM

Arsenal

v Manchester United (h)	won 1–0
v Aston Villa (h)	won 1–0
v West Ham (a)	won 2–1
v Manchester City (h)	won 5–0

THE TOP...

Team	Pld	W	D	L	F	A	GD	Pts
1 Manchester United	15	11	3	1	39	10	+29	36
2 Arsenal	15	8	4	3	22	13	+10	28
3 Ipswich Town	15	8	3	4	23	16	+7	27

THE BOTTOM...

Team	Pld	W	D	L	F	A	GD	Pts
18 Middlesbrough	15	2	5	8	19	26	-7	11
19 Derby County	15	1	7	7	18	31	-13	10
20 Bradford City	15	1	5	9	7	24	-17	8

PLAYER OF THE MONTH

Mart Poom, Goalkeeper, Derby County

Mins on pitch	360

Goals

Goals conceded	3
Clean sheets	3

Saves

Inside box	9
Outside box	11
Saves-to-shots ratio	87%

FORM TEAM

West Ham

v Derby County (a)	drew 0–0
v Manchester City (h)	won 4–1
v Leeds United (a)	won 1–0
v Southampton (a)	won 3–2

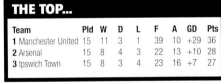

THE PREMIERSHIP

DECEMBER

After plenty of will he, won't he rumours, Terry Venables finally arrives at Teeside – at least temporarily, although he insists he remains committed to his job at ITV and is only helping Bryan Robson in his fight against relegation.

THE TOP...

Team	Pld	W	D	L	F	A	GD	Pts
1 Manchester United	21	14	5	2	48	15	+33	47
2 Arsenal	21	11	6	4	38	21	+17	39
3 Ipswich Town	21	11	4	6	32	22	+10	37

THE BOTTOM...

Team	Pld	W	D	L	F	A	GD	Pts
18 Middlesbrough	21	4	7	10	22	29	-7	19
19 Manchester City	21	5	4	12	26	37	-11	19
20 Bradford City	20	2	6	12	14	37	-23	12

PLAYER OF THE MONTH

Thierry Henry, Striker, Arsenal

Mins on pitch	469
Goal Attempts	
Goals	4
Shots on target	19
Shots off target	9
Blocked shots	5
Goals-to-shots ratio	12%

FORM TEAM

Sunderland

v Everton (h)	won 2–0
v Middlesbrough (h)	won 1–0
v Leeds United (a)	lost 0–2
v Manchester City (h)	won 1–0
v Bradford City (a)	won 4–1
v Arsenal (a)	drew 2–2

Results at Middlesbrough begin to pick up.

Leeds United offer £10m for Robbie Keane, despite the insistence that he's happy at Internazionale. David O'Leary's team continue their excellent run in Europe, with a 1–0 win over Lazio in Rome, that sparks rumours that Sven's permanent appointment as England coach may start sooner than previously expected.

Back in the Premiership, the row between the Hammers star Paolo Di Canio and Aston Villa goalkeeper David James reaches boiling point after the penalty drama of last year's Worthington Cup. The Italian describes James as a "cretin". James responds with: "A cretin suffers from dwarfism... I'm 6'5" for goodness sake." Although, heart-warmingly, the players subsequently make up.

A number of big names suffer injury problems. Graeme Le Saux breaks down again in training and Alan Shearer discovers his long-awaited knee operation will put him out for the season. At Aston Villa, John Gregory accuses David Ginola of carrying a bit of extra weight. Ginola responds by scoring in the following match and ripping his shirt off to reveal admirably toned stomach muscles.

Never the silent type, Gregory also accuses Villa chairman "Deadly" Doug Ellis of being "small time" and "living in a time warp". Although, before matters can get too heated, Gregory takes the sensible step of rapidly backtracking, and apologises to his employer.

JANUARY

Manchester United continue to dominate the top of the table. A 3–1 win against West Ham opens up an 11-point lead, and the rest of the league seem to resign themselves to chasing second place. Arsene Wenger is quoted in the tabloids insisting that his club has to buy big if they're to have any chance of catching up with United, but no new signings are announced. However, Tony Adams announces his retirement from international football to concentrate on his club career. "I owe it to Arsenal to end my England career now," he says.

On the other side of north London, Tottenham aren't looking too healthy. Despite claiming he wants to stay at the club, Sol Campbell still doesn't sign a new deal and rumours continue to link him to other clubs, home and abroad. With something of an injury crisis at White Hart Lane, the club bring in non-scoring striker Andy Booth on a month's loan from Sheffield Wednesday. Alan Sugar announces he is ending his not-always-popular ten-year reign at Spurs, handing over control to ENIC.

Meanwhile, Liverpool sign Finnish international Jari Litmanen on a free transfer and Mark Bosnich finally ends his Manchester United nightmare and moves to Chelsea. "I can't express how grateful I am to Chelsea for giving me this chance," says Bozzie. But he is not immediately made first-choice keeper.

West Ham striker Jermaine Defoe is causing a stir on loan to Bournemouth. The 18-year-old, scores 12 goals in ten games for the club, setting a post-war record.

A radio DJ fools Sven-Goran Eriksson by pretending to be Kevin Keegan and discovers that the Swede plans to make David Beckham his captain for the foreseeable future.

THE TOP...

Team	Pld	W	D	L	F	A	GD	Pts
1 Manchester United	28	18	5	2	57	16	+41	59
2 Arsenal	25	12	8	5	41	23	+18	44
3 Sunderland	25	12	7	6	31	23	+8	43

THE BOTTOM...

Team	Pld	W	D	L	F	A	GD	Pts
18 Manchester City	25	5	7	13	29	44	-15	22
19 Coventry City	25	5	6	14	23	44	-21	21
20 Bradford City	24	3	7	14	16	43	-27	16

PLAYER OF THE MONTH

Steven Gerrard, Midfielder, Liverpool

Mins on pitch	270
Passing	
Goal Assists	4
Total passes	228
Pass completion	77%
Defending	
Tackles made	19
Tackles won	84%
Blocks	3
Clearances	14
Interceptions	1

FORM TEAM

Manchester United

v West Ham United (h)	won 3–1
v Bradford City (a)	won 3–0
v Aston Villa (h)	won 2–0
v Sunderland (a)	won 1–0

FEBRUARY

Arsene Wenger receives a £10,000 fine and is reprimanded for improper conduct after touching Paul Taylor in the match against Sunderland on the opening day of the season.

John Hartson finally leaves Wimbledon for Coventry on a pay-as-you-play basis. The Welsh hitman who in recent months had come close to joining Spurs and Rangers, heads to Highfield Road to try and help the Sky Blues in their bid to avoid relegation.

Meanwhile Bruce Grobbelaar, who is continuing the fight to clear his name after bribe allegations, claims his dream is still to coach football in England, "I dream of going to coach in Europe and England once I have done my apprenticeship here in Africa," he says. "The dream is still alive, and it will carry on until the Lord takes my life away."

Manchester United fans don't need to dream. They're walking on air after an astonishing 6-1 thrashing over perennial title rivals Arsenal. The supposedly off-form striker Dwight Yorke scores a stunning hat-trick.

"I've had a frustrating season up until now," admits Yorke. "But I made sure I kept myself fit and sharp because I knew if my chance did come I would have to take it. There was a bit of pressure on me, but I was really determined. It was fantastic to get a hat-trick in such a big game. I felt my confidence flooding back."

Ole Gunnar Solskjaer, Teddy Sheringham and Roy Keane also get on the scoresheet to pile on the agony for the Gunners. An embarassed Arsene Wenger is forced to admit: "We are not yet in March and the title race is over. You cannot be proud of that."

MARCH

Stuart Pearce is voted Carling Player of the Month for February, making him the first person to win both Carling Player and Manager of the Month awards. The 38-year-old is also the oldest player ever to have scooped the Player of the Month accolade.

Also getting honours, Newcastle United striker Alan Shearer is given the key to the city of Newcastle by the Mayor at a special ceremony.

Shearer's current replacement as England striker, Andy Cole, breaks his international goal scoring duck by striking in injury-time to seal a 3–1 victory over the Albanians in Tirana. His team-mate David Beckham scores the winner in a tight 2–1 victory over the Finns at Anfield, to cap an impressive all round performance from England's burgeoning young side.

It means Sven-Goran Eriksson's first two competitive games in charge of the national side have gone pretty smoothly as England pick up maximum points to put their World Cup qualifying campaign back on track after a disappointing start.

Following the resignation of Glenn Hoddle, first-team coach Stuart Gray is appointed manager of Southampton for the remainder of the season.

At Elland Road, Brian Kidd is unveiled as Leeds' new first-team coach, moving from his previous position as Academy Director. Kiddo makes the move just in time to sit on the bench for Leeds' home match against his former team Manchester United. The game finishes honours even at 1–1.

THE TOP...

Team	Pld	W	D	L	F	A	GD	Pts
1 Manchester United	28	20	6	2	65	18	+47	66
2 Arsenal	28	14	8	6	44	29	+15	50
3 Liverpool	26	13	6	7	47	28	+19	45

THE BOTTOM...

Team	Pld	W	D	L	F	A	GD	Pts
18 Manchester City	28	6	8	14	31	46	-15	26
19 Coventry City	28	5	8	15	26	48	-22	23
20 Bradford City	27	3	7	17	17	50	-33	16

PLAYER OF THE MONTH

Dwight Yorke, Striker, Manchester United

Mins of pitch	165

Goals Attempts

Goals	3
Shots on target	4
Shots off target	2
Blocked shots	0
Goals-to-shots ratio	50%

FORM TEAM

Leeds United

v Ipswich Town (a)	won 2–1
v Everton (a)	drew 2–2
v Derby County (h)	drew 0–0
v Tottenham Hotspur (a)	won 2–1

THE TOP...

Team	Pld	W	D	L	F	A	GD	Pts
1 Manchester United	31	21	7	3	68	21	+47	70
2 Arsenal	31	16	9	6	49	29	+20	57
3 Leeds United	31	14	8	9	46	38	+8	50

THE BOTTOM...

Team	Pld	W	D	L	F	A	GD	Pts
18 Manchester City	31	6	9	16	34	52	-18	27
19 Coventry City	31	6	9	16	28	51	-23	27
20 Bradford City	30	3	9	18	22	57	-35	18

PLAYER OF THE MONTH

Martijn Reuser, Midfielder, Ipswich Town

Mins on pitch	256

Crossing

Total crosses	39
Cross completion	28%

Dribbling

Dribbles and runs	11
Dribble completion	73%

FORM TEAM

Aston Villa

v Sunderland (a)	drew 1–1
v Ipswich Town (h)	won 2–1
v Arsenal (h)	drew 0–0
v Manchester City (a)	won 3–1

Ferguson admits: "I really didn't expect Arsenal to lose at home at all. I was still at Old Trafford with a few friends who'd come down from Scotland. When we heard the half-time score from Highbury was 2–0 to Boro, we decided to stay on! It's still great winning the Premiership – it is the hardest league in the world to win."

Although defeat in Europe has tempered the United celebrations. As Gary Neville observes: "Three in a row is a significant achievement and in any other season we'd probably have been jumping for joy, but with our standards being set at a certain level now it's become that the title isn't the be all and end all. It's the European Cup that drives us and is what we're judged on. The disappointment from that is at the forefront of people's minds."

However, there is more cause for celebration at the club when Teddy Sheringham is declared the winner of both the PFA Player of the Year award and the Football Writers' equivalent.

Arriving in time for the party is new signing, Dutch striker Ruud van Nistelrooy, whose on-off deal is finally completed for a cool £19 million.

Leeds also get out the cheque book, spending £11 million to secure the services of Robbie Keane who spent the majority of the season at Elland Road on loan.

The trial of Leeds United's Lee Bowyer and Jonathan Woodgate collapses. Meanwhile, Everton's Ghanaian international, Alex Nyarko, swears to retire from football following an irate fan's persistent jibes which culminate with him approaching Nyarko on the pitch at Arsenal. The fan seemed to offer the midfield man an exchange of shirts.

APRIL

Manchester United win the Premiership title for the third time in a row, as Fulham clinch promotion to the top flight.

Arsenal's surprise 0–3 home defeat against Boro is the result that ensures the title will go to Old Trafford yet again, although Sir Alex

THE TOP...

Team	Pld	W	D	L	F	A	GD	Pts
1 Manchester United	35	24	8	3	77	25	+52	80
2 Arsenal	35	19	9	7	59	34	+25	66
3 Leeds United	35	18	8	9	54	39	+15	62

THE BOTTOM...

Team	Pld	W	D	L	F	A	GD	Pts
18 Manchester City	36	8	10	18	39	61	-22	34
19 Coventry City	36	8	9	19	34	60	-26	33
20 Bradford City	34	5	9	20	28	61	-33	24

PLAYER OF THE MONTH

Fredrik Ljungberg, Midfielder, Arsenal

Mins on pitch	334

Goals

Goals	3
Shots on target	9
Shots off target	3
Blocked shots	2
Goals-to-shots ratio	21%

Dribbles

Dribbles and runs	26
Dribble completion	81%

FORM TEAM

Ipswich Town

v Southampton (a)	won 3–0
v Liverpool (h)	drew 1–1
v Newcastle United (h)	won 1–0
v Middlesbrough (a)	won 2–1
v Coventry City (h)	won 2–0
v Charlton Athletic (a)	lost 1–2

MAY

With the title already Old Trafford-bound, the big issues in the Premiership concern who's going to secure the other two Champions League qualifying spots and who is for the drop.

On the former, Arsenal soon secure second spot but Leeds, Liverpool and Ipswich are neck and neck for third. Things are resolved in Anfield's favour on the last day of the season with an emphatic 4–0 away victory at Charlton.

Leeds put a brave face on missing out: "It will help us concentrate on winning the championship next season," insists chairman Peter Ridsdale.

Ipswich are cheered by the announcement that George Burley has won Carling's Manager of the Year award.

There's little for Manchester City, Coventry and Bradford to celebrate though as all three teams slip out of the top flight. City manager, Joe Royle, leaves and is replaced by Kevin Keegan.

Surprisingly, there is also talk of managerial departures at Old Trafford with the press making much of an apparent rift between Ferguson and the plc board. For the first time in years, United are not odds-on to win the title next season!

PLAYER OF THE MONTH

Kevin Phillips, Striker, Sunderland

Mins on pitch	180

Goal Attempts

Goals	3
Shots on target	10
Shots off target	5
Blocked shots	0
Goals-to-shots ratio	20%

FORM TEAM

Liverpool

v Bradford City (a)	won 2–0
v Newcastle United (h)	won 3–0
v Chelsea (h)	drew 2–2
v Charlton Athletic (a)	won 4–0

Champions again! Sir Alex Ferguson leads his team to a third successive title triumph.

FINAL PREMIERSHIP TABLE

	HOME						AWAY					Pts
	P	W	D	L	F	A	W	D	L	F	A	
Manchester United	38	15	2	2	49	12	9	6	4	30	19	80
Arsenal	38	15	3	1	45	13	5	7	7	18	25	70
Liverpool	38	13	4	2	40	14	7	5	7	31	25	69
Leeds United	38	11	3	5	36	21	9	5	5	28	22	68
Ipswich Town	38	11	5	3	31	15	9	1	9	26	27	66
Chelsea	38	13	3	3	44	20	4	7	8	24	25	61
Sunderland	38	9	7	3	24	16	6	5	8	22	25	57
Aston Villa	38	8	8	3	27	20	5	7	7	19	23	54
Charlton Athletic	38	11	5	3	31	19	3	5	11	19	38	52
Southampton	38	11	2	6	27	22	3	8	8	13	26	52
Newcastle United	38	10	4	5	26	17	4	5	10	18	33	51
Tottenham Hotspur	38	11	6	2	31	16	2	4	13	16	38	49
Leicester City	38	10	4	5	28	23	4	2	13	11	28	48
Middlesbrough	38	4	7	8	18	23	5	8	6	26	21	42
West Ham United	38	6	6	7	24	20	4	6	9	21	30	42
Everton	38	6	8	5	29	27	5	1	13	16	32	42
Derby County	38	8	7	4	23	24	2	5	12	14	35	42
Manchester City	38	4	3	12	20	31	4	7	8	21	34	34
Coventry City	38	4	7	8	14	23	4	3	12	22	40	34
Bradford City	38	4	7	8	20	29	1	4	14	10	41	26

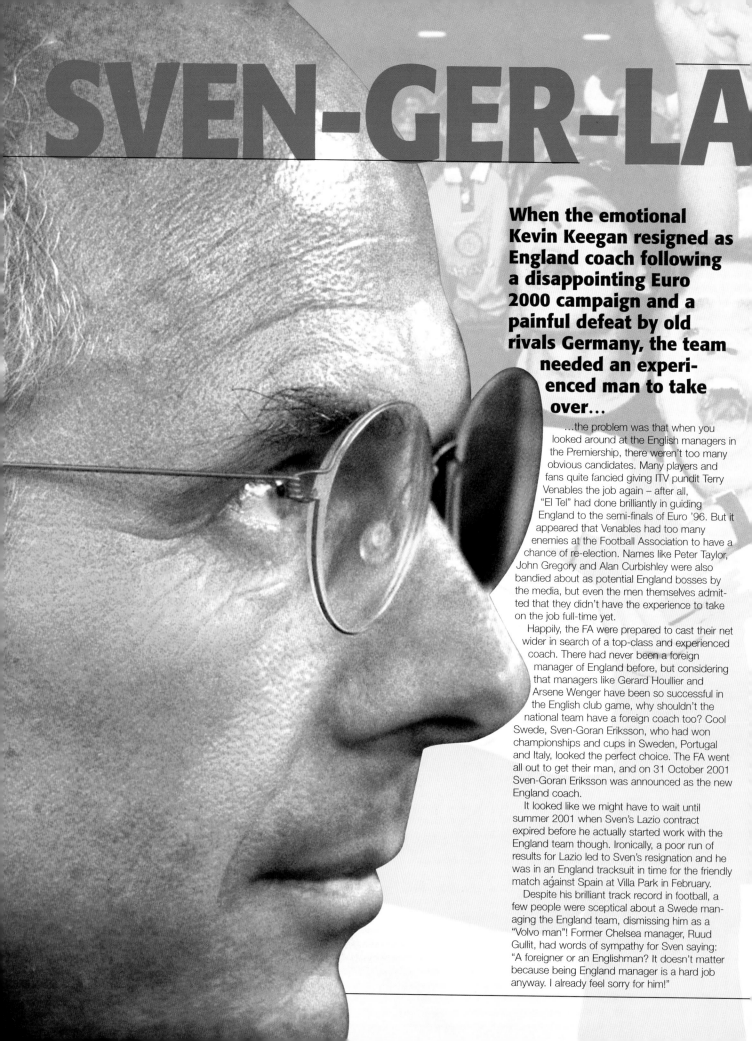

SVEN-GER-LA

When the emotional Kevin Keegan resigned as England coach following a disappointing Euro 2000 campaign and a painful defeat by old rivals Germany, the team needed an experienced man to take over...

...the problem was that when you looked around at the English managers in the Premiership, there weren't too many obvious candidates. Many players and fans quite fancied giving ITV pundit Terry Venables the job again – after all, "El Tel" had done brilliantly in guiding England to the semi-finals of Euro '96. But it appeared that Venables had too many enemies at the Football Association to have a chance of re-election. Names like Peter Taylor, John Gregory and Alan Curbishley were also bandied about as potential England bosses by the media, but even the men themselves admitted that they didn't have the experience to take on the job full-time yet.

Happily, the FA were prepared to cast their net wider in search of a top-class and experienced coach. There had never been a foreign manager of England before, but considering that managers like Gerard Houllier and Arsene Wenger have been so successful in the English club game, why shouldn't the national team have a foreign coach too? Cool Swede, Sven-Goran Eriksson, who had won championships and cups in Sweden, Portugal and Italy, looked the perfect choice. The FA went all out to get their man, and on 31 October 2001 Sven-Goran Eriksson was announced as the new England coach.

It looked like we might have to wait until summer 2001 when Sven's Lazio contract expired before he actually started work with the England team though. Ironically, a poor run of results for Lazio led to Sven's resignation and he was in an England tracksuit in time for the friendly match against Spain at Villa Park in February.

Despite his brilliant track record in football, a few people were sceptical about a Swede managing the England team, dismissing him as a "Volvo man"! Former Chelsea manager, Ruud Gullit, had words of sympathy for Sven saying: "A foreigner or an Englishman? It doesn't matter because being England manager is a hard job anyway. I already feel sorry for him!"

ND!

Sven gets to know David James, David Beckham and Frank Lampard .

"Mr Grimsdale!" Some nutter approaches Sven.

But Sven's charming manner and a promising 3–0 win over Spain in his first match did much to shut the critics up. Even the Spanish manager, Jose Camacho, was impressed commenting afterwards that, "We are not at England's level."

Two consecutive wins in World Cup matches (2–1 against Finland at Anfield and 3–1 away to Albania) followed to lift England from bottom of the group to second position and showed Sven was bonding well with his new team. Rather than start a revolution, Sven seems determined to build on the strengths of English football. A great lover of the pass-and-move style used by the brilliant Liverpool teams of the late 1970s and early '80s, Sven wanted his new captain David Beckham and his colleagues to express themselves freely.

Hmm... Peter Taylor joins Sven in some heavy-duty pondering.

Give that man a medal! Sven obliges.

"I have always thought that the most important thing was the players and not the system you play," he said.

And, boy, did he see some players in his first few months in charge. You could hardly watch a Premiership game on telly without spotting Sven or his right-hand man, Tord Grip, making notes in the crowd. Such dedication paid off and he uncovered some useful players who had been ignored by past managers. For instance, it had often been said that we had no left-footed players in this country and yet Sven miraculously found five left-footers to put in his first squad including 31-year-old Charlton full back, Chris Powell, who started against Spain and looked the part.

So a good start for Sven then, but like English England managers before him, the Swede will be judged on his results. If things go wrong, fans and the press can be very cruel – poor old Graham Taylor was turned into a turnip. Let's hope balding Sven can lead England to the World Cup finals and avoid being morphed into his "Simpsons" cartoon look-a-like Mr Burns!

"Now listen up..." Sven gives a team-talk.

"After you..."
"No, after you..."

"These sleeves are far too long..."

THE LIFE & TIMES OF SVEN

1948 On 5 February, Sven is born in Torsby, Sweden.
1975 A serious knee injury brings 27-year-old Sven's playing career with Swedish second division side Karlskoga to an a premature end.
1976 Sven shows his flair for coaching at Swedish club Degerfors. He leads them from the third division to the first division in three years
1980–82 Joins IFK Gothenburg where he wins a Swedish championship, two

domestic cups and the 1982 UEFA Cup.
1982–84 Sven's golden touch continues at Benfica where he wins two championships in two seasons.
1984–87 He dips his toe into Italian football for the first time as coach of AS Roma. In his second season, Roma are pipped in the title race by Juventus but win the Italian Cup.
1987–89 Sven resigns from Roma in May 1987 and coaches Fiorentina to eighth- and seventh-place finishes in Serie A.

1989–91 Does brilliantly on his return to Benfica guiding them to the 1990 European Cup final and the 1991 Portuguese league title.
1991–96 Back in Italy with Sampdoria, Sven suffers a lean spell, only winning one trophy (the Italian Cup) in five years.
1997/98 Arrives at Lazio and coaches the team to an Italian Cup victory in his first season.
1998/99 Lazio win the Cup Winners' Cup, the club's first ever European

trophy, but they just miss out on the Serie A championship – finishing one point behind AC Milan.
1999/2000 Sven's crowning glory – he leads Lazio to a league and cup double. The Serie A triumph is the club's first for 26 years. In October 2000, Sven is confirmed as the next England coach after Kevin Keegan's resignation.
2001 On 9 January, Sven resigns as Lazio coach and takes charge of the Three Lions.

MAGIC M

Leeds United were just fantastic in last year's Champions League. For me, Alan Smith's 80th-minute winner against Lazio at the Olympic Stadium last December summed up their spirit, skill and fighting qualities. Real Madrid had beaten them easily in the first match of the second phase, but not for the first time in the tournament, they bounced back with a superb victory. It was a beautifully worked goal too. Mark Viduka's sublime back-flick put Smith in and he finished off the move as cool as you like.

OMENTS

No 1: Gabby Yorath

7

STYLE FILE

Pineapple Head, Jason Lee took plenty of stick for his hair "style". But Becks set a trend for the nation's youth with his designer mohican!

Perm-a-rific! Arsenal's Alan Sunderland and England's Kevin Keegan were real trendsetters with their bubble perms.

Red alert! Freddie Ljungberg and Jamie Lawrence are happy to go for the traffic-light look.

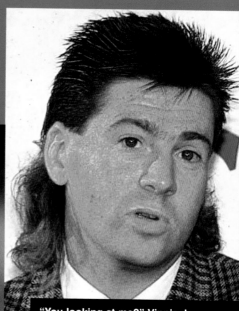

Eek! No wonder Carlos Valderrama looks disgusted. He's just caught sight of himself in the mirror!

"You looking at me?" Vinnie Jones goes for a short, sharp, hard man crop. Chris Waddle prefers a more mullet-tastic approach.

MEN IN BLACK

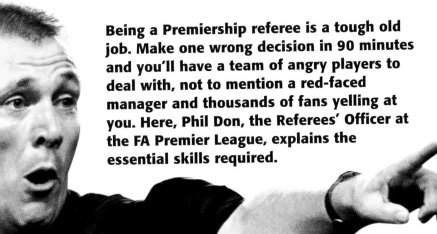

Being a Premiership referee is a tough old job. Make one wrong decision in 90 minutes and you'll have a team of angry players to deal with, not to mention a red-faced manager and thousands of fans yelling at you. Here, Phil Don, the Referees' Officer at the FA Premier League, explains the essential skills required.

So if a player commits a foul, a referee may just give a free-kick and have a quiet word with the player as the game continues. If that doesn't work, he can try giving the player a more public telling-off and if the player still isn't listening then you get into yellow and red cards."

▓ IT'S GOOD TO TALK…

"Communication between the referee and players is very important. A lot of that talking goes on while the game is in progress and it goes unnoticed by normal spectators or journalists, but I look for it when I'm assessing a referee's performance."

▓ GET THE BIG DECISIONS RIGHT!

"A ref can be having a great game but one mistake and all the good work goes out of the window. We stress to referees that they've got to get the major decisions right. People don't mind if you miss the odd push or shove, but you've got to be spot on with things like a penalty or sending-off decision. Because of the pace of the game now, the ref is bound to be caught out of position occasionally, so we expect assistant refs to get more involved – they aren't just linesmen any more."

▓ MANAGE THE GAME

"You must know the 17 laws of football no matter at what level you officiate. But top referees know how to manage the game and the players within those laws. It's getting the balance right so that not every foul is a booking. For example, Paul Durkin, who is one of our best refs, showed very few yellow cards last season."

▓ THE FIVE–STEP PUNISHMENT

"In the last 18 months we've given back referees the power to use their discretion.

▓ YOU GOTTA BE FIT

"Premier League refs must pass a fitness test at the start of the season and then they do another three fitness assessments through the year. We set them targets and design a fitness programme for them based on the results. We even analyse their diet."

▓ DEDICATION'S WHAT YOU NEED

"Refs don't just turn up at 2pm on a Saturday and go home at five. Most Premiership referees have other jobs but still put in around 30 hours a week into their refereeing if you include the training, travel and matches. And of the 20 Premier League referees, nine are on the international list so they often have to go on three-day trips abroad too."

▓ GAME FOR A LAUGH

"If you are going to be offended by the comments made by fans and players, you may as well give up. You've got to have a thick skin and a sense of humour. To me, what marks out an outstanding ref from a good one is his composure. Watch a top referee and he is always calm under pressure, doesn't get flustered or show anger… even if they are really fed up!"

YOU'RE JOKING, REF!

Which refs waved the most cards in the 2000/01 Premiership season...				
REFEREE	Matches	Yellow cards	Red cards	Bookings per per game
Graham Barber	19	91	2	4.79
Mike Riley	20	87	1	4.35
Rob Styles	17	65	4	3.82
Barry Knight	16	61	6	3.81
Peter Jones	16	59	2	3.69
Rob Harris	13	46	2	3.54
Andy D'Urso	21	71	6	3.38
Clive Wilkes	9	30	0	3.33
Matt Messias	3	30	0	3.33
Mike Dean	18	57	1	3.17
David Elleray	21	66	3	3.14
Dermot Gallagher	20	62	4	3.10
Mark Halsey	16	49	1	3.06
Graham Poll	24	72	8	3.00
Steve Lodge	18	52	1	2.89
Paul Taylor	13	37	1	2.85
Jeff Winter	22	62	3	2.82
Neale Barry	18	49	3	2.72
Steve Bennett	17	45	5	2.65
Steve Dunn	19	50	2	2.63
Alan Wiley	25	62	2	2.48
Paul Durkin	23	47	2	2.04

WORTHINGTON

FIRST ROUND

There were some high-scoring encounters as soon as the competition kicked off. Blackburn Rovers smashed six past Rochdale, including a hat-trick of penalties from David Dunn, while Sheffield United put six past Lincoln and Birmingham City began their cup bid with a 5–0 thrashing of Southend United. Meanwhile Chesterfield and Wycombe both needed extra-time to book their places in the second round.

SECOND ROUND

The second round saw the arrival of some of the Premiership big boys, although they didn't all last long. Charlton went out 4–3 on aggregate to Stoke City and Everton didn't fare any better, losing on away goals to Bristol Rovers. Bradford City were the big scorers, with a 7–2 win over Darlington, and Sheffield Wednesday stuck five past Oldham. Birmingham City's run continued with a 5–3 aggregate win over Wycombe.

Many Premier League giants were slain at the third round stage.

THIRD ROUND

More Premiership hot shots arrived on the scene. Manchester United eased into the next round with a 3–0 win over Watford, but Chelsea were drawn against Liverpool and went out in extra-time to a late winner by Robbie Fowler. Southampton, Arsenal, Aston Villa, Middlesbrough and Leicester were other teams from the top flight to get knocked out although the biggest shock was the exit of Leeds. David O'Leary's side went out 3–2 in extra-time to Tranmere Rovers. Birmingham City's excellent away win at Spurs kept their hopes alive.

FOURTH ROUND

Anyone who thought this was the season Manchester United might actually make a real run in the competition soon had those thoughts quashed as Alex Ferguson's boys went out at their second hurdle. To be fair, they did take Sunderland to extra-time before a Kevin Phillips penalty settled matters. Tranmere Rovers' run also came to an end in a penalty shoot-out thriller that Crystal Palace edged 6–5. There was more drama at Craven Cottage, as Fulham's Louis Saha snatched a 90th-minute winner in the 3–2 victory over Derby. Things weren't so tight between Stoke and Liverpool. Gerard Houllier's men romped to a 8–0 win and Robbie Fowler grabbed a hat-trick. Birmingham's impressive run continued with victory over Newcastle, and Ipswich, Manchester City and Sheffield Wednesday made up the final eight.

QUARTER-FINALS

The pick of the quarters was the mouth-watering prospect of Jean Tigana's excellent Fulham side taking on Liverpool at Anfield. For 90 minutes, there was little between the two sides and the game went into extra-time scoreless. But then Liverpool stepped up a gear and goals from Michael Owen, Vladimir Smicer and Nick Barmby settled the tie convincingly. Manchester City sniffed a semi-final opportunity after Shaun Goater gave them a tenth-minute lead against Ipswich, but Matty Holland's second-half

Super Kev ended the hopes of Manchester United's "B team".

Liverpool's Premiership class eventually told against Jean Tigana's Fulham.

Brum fans and players celebrate the shock semi-final win over Ipswich.

CUP

win against Sheffield Wednesday.

SEMI-FINALS

An all-Premiership final looked a possibility when Ipswich and Liverpool managed to avoid each other in the draw. But Crystal Palace had other plans and beat the Merseysiders 2–1 in the first leg. However, it was a rather different story at Anfield as Vladimir Smicer, Danny Murphy, Igor Biscan and Robbie Fowler all got on the scoresheet in a convincing 5–0 hammering. Gerald Houllier's men were in the final! But would Ipswich join them? After a 1–0 victory over Birmingham in the first leg, you would have thought so. But City weren't going to let their cup-run end now. Martin Grainger and Geoff Horsfield got the goals to give them a 2–1 aggregate lead on the night and a place in the final beckoned. There was still time for a little more drama though. Jamie Scowcroft hit back for Ipswich to make the aggregate score 2–2. Not for the first time, it was all going to be down to extra-time. Horsfield struck in the 107th minute to put Trevor Francis' team back in the driving seat, and Andy Johnson made certain of victory with three minutes left. Birmingham had made it!

THE FINAL

Liverpool started the final at the Millennium Stadium as overwhelming favourites. Everything appeared to be following the script when Robbie Fowler gave Liverpool an early lead, but the Anfield side were unable to build on it. Sure enough, in the dying seconds of the game, Liverpool got a nasty surprise. Martin O'Connor was flattened by defender Stephane Henchoz and the referee pointed to the spot. Penalty! Darren Purse cooly slotted the ball home to take the final into extra-time. Sadly, for Trevor Francis' men, it wasn't enough. A penalty shoot-out was required and with the score poised at 4–4, Sander Westerveld saved Andy Johnson's penalty to clinch Liverpool's first trophy win of the season!

equaliser took the game into extra-time and Mark Venus finished things off with a winner in the 109th minute. Crystal Palace made the last four after a tussle with Sunderland. It was all square with eight minutes remaining but then Clinton Morrison gave the Londoners victory. Birmingham City, on the other hand, glided into the semi-finals with a straightforward 2–0 home

Liverpool were big favourites but Birmingham City never gave up.

ROUND 3

Southampton 0	Coventry City 1
Arsenal 1	Ipswich Town 2
Aston Villa 0	Manchester City 1
Wimbledon 1	Middlesbrough 0
Tottenham Hotspur 1	Birmingham City 3
Newcastle United 4	Bradford City 3
Sheffield Wednesday 2	Sheffield United 1
West Ham United 2	Blackburn Rovers 0
Stoke City 3	Barnsley 2
Liverpool 2	Chelsea 1
Derby County 3	Norwich City 0
Fulham 3	Wolverhampton Wanderers 2
Leicester City 0	Crystal Palace 3
Tranmere Rovers 3	Leeds United 2
Bristol Rovers 1	Sunderland 2
Watford 0	Manchester United 3

ROUND 4

Birmingham City 2	Newcastle United 1
Crystal Palace 0	Tranmere Rovers 0
Crystal Palace win 6–5 on penalties	
Fulham 3	Derby County 2
Ipswich Town 2	Coventry City 1
Manchester City 2	Wimbledon 1
Stoke City 0	Liverpool 8
Sunderland 2	Manchester United 1
West Ham United 1	Sheffield Wednesday 2

QUARTER-FINALS

Manchester City 1	Ipswich Town 2
Birmingham City 2	Sheffield Wednesday 0
Liverpool 3	Fulham 0
Crystal Palace 2	Sunderland 1

SEMI-FINALS first leg

Ipswich Town 1	Birmingham City 0
Crystal Palace 2	Liverpool 1

SEMI-FINALS second leg

Liverpool 5	Crystal Palace 0
Liverpool win 6–2 on aggregate	
Birmingham City 4	Ipswich Town 1
Birmingham win 4–2 on aggregate	

FINAL

Birmingham City 1	Liverpool 1
After extra-time, Liverpool win 5–4 on penalties	

Liverpool wasted a lot of good champagne in 2001!

WHO CAN REPLACE SIR FERGIE?

Sir Alex Ferguson says he's retiring at the end of the season. But who else could take on one of the biggest jobs in football? And what special qualities would they need? We investigate.

After over a decade of success, "The Gaffer" is off. Alex Ferguson has stated that this will definitely be his last season as manager of Manchester United. But whoever takes over from him has got an awful lot to live up to. After all, under Ferguson, United have become the most successful team in the country, and one of the most successful in the world. League Championships, FA Cups, Doubles, Double doubles and even the Treble have all come United's way under their Scottish boss. And not forgetting a League Cup, European Cup Winners' Cup and Club World Championship as well!

Last season, they practically walked the Championship, opening up a gap on Arsenal, Liverpool and the rest that was simply huge. And you can be sure they'll be looking for even more silverware in Ferguson's last season.

So what's the secret of their success? Well, for a start, there's loyalty. When Ferguson first arrived at Old Trafford, the trophies didn't come straight away but the club persevered with their man when some were calling for his head. The result was stability and consistent success. Then there's the youth policy. While other teams have spent for-tunes on big name signings to try and catch United, the Reds have brought through a lot of their best players from the ranks of their own youngsters. Ryan Giggs, David Beckham, Paul

Scholes, Wes Brown, the Nevilles, Nicky Butt, Luke Chadwick… the list goes on. And when United have dipped into the transfer market, they've made some of the best signings ever. Eric Cantona, Peter Schmeichel, Roy Keane, Jaap Stam and Fabien Barthez to name but a few.

On top of all that, Ferguson has injected a special quality into all his players: hunger. It doesn't matter how often his team win, they always seem to want more success. The simple fact is that they've been more consistently "up for it" than any of their rivals, week-in, week-out.

But will the good times continue after Fergie's gone? Ever since he announced he was leaving, the papers have been full of speculation about who could follow in his footsteps. Some say the job should go to Steve McClaren, others have suggested United should poach one of the Premiership's other high-fliers, like David O'Leary, Alan Curbishley or George Burley. Then there's the school of thought that think Old Trafford needs a European to ensure Champions League success. Johan Cruyff, Marcello Lippi, Fabio Capello and even Fulham's Jean Tigana have been mentioned. And finally, there's Martin O'Neill. The Celtic boss is favourite for the job, even though no-one's sure if he actually wants it!

So who's going to get it? Er, don't know. But we do reckon it will probably be one of the people featured on this page...

THE CANDIDATES

MARTIN O'NEILL
A European Cup winner with Nottingham Forest as a player, O'Neill has guided Wycombe Wanderers, Leicester City and most recently Celtic to great success.

Experience
Man management
Tactics

STEVE McCLAREN
Earned rave reviews for his training methods at Derby before Fergie took him on. Has the advantage of knowing the United players inside out.

Experience
Man management
Tactics

DAVID O'LEARY
David took over as manager of Leeds United after George Graham left and led a young team to the Champions League semi-final.

Experience
Man management
Tactics

JOHAN CRUYFF
Has coached Ajax to European Cup Winners' Cup success and lead Barcelona to four League titles and the European Cup. The only doubt is his health.

Experience
Man management
Tactics

MARCELLO LIPPI
Lippi's greatest successes were at Juventus where he won Serie A, the European Cup, the European Super Cup and the World Club Cup.

Experience
Man management
Tactics

FABIO CAPELLO
Won three successive Italian titles and the European Cup with AC Milan before going to Real Madrid and winning the League in his first (and only) season there.

Experience
Man management
Tactics

ALAN CURBISHLEY
A loyal servant to Charlton Athletic, Alan has built them up from a struggling Nationwide side into one of the most attractive teams to watch in England.

Experience
Man management
Tactics

JEAN TIGANA
The former French international midfielder coached Monaco to the French League title. He then moved to Fulham and promptly led them back to the Premiership.

Experience
Man management
Tactics

GEORGE BURLEY
Confounded everyone's expectations by not only making newly-promoted Ipswich survive in the Premiership but flourish. The Scot is a manager on the up.

Experience
Man management
Tactics

YOUNG LIONS!

Some people complain that the Premiership has too many foreign footballers which makes it hard for English players to break through. But if a young Lion has the talent, he can make it in Europe's most exciting league as the six players featured here have proved. Let's take a closer look at the future of English football…

WES BROWN

Age: 21 Position: Defender

Hailed by pundits as "the new Bobby Moore", Wes makes defending look preposterously easy. From the final day of the 1997/98 season when he made his Manchester United debut at Barnsley, his ability was immediately apparent and he became the fastest-ever capped England player when Kevin Keegan gave him his international debut in Hungary after having played just 11 Premiership matches.

Laid-back Wes is a composed defender and his comfort on the ball makes him equally effective whether he's playing in the centre of defence or as a full back. He showed guts to overcome a serious knee injury in 1999/2000 and his next challenge is to try and displace Rio Ferdinand or Sol Campbell at the heart of England's defence.

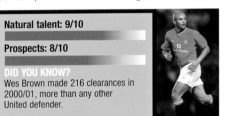

Natural talent: 9/10

Prospects: 8/10

DID YOU KNOW?
Wes Brown made 216 clearances in 2000/01, more than any other United defender.

ASHLEY COLE

Age: 20 Position: Defender

A graduate from Arsenal's Centre Of Excellence, East Londoner Ashley made a huge impact in 2000/01. It's a measure of Ashley's prodigious ability that he made over 30 starts for Arsenal last season where he is competing against brilliant Brazilian Silvinho for the left-back slot. His sound defensive skills and ability to roam forward and supply dangerous crosses has clearly caught the attention of Sven-Goran Eriksson. After taking over as England boss, Eriksson immediately called Cole into the full international squad.

Cole has been earmarked for great things since helping Arsenal's youth side to the FA Premier Youth league title in 1998. Now he has made the step up to international level, England's search for a top-quality left-back is surely over.

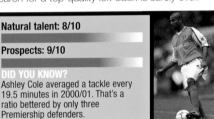

Natural talent: 8/10

Prospects: 9/10

DID YOU KNOW?
Ashley Cole averaged a tackle every 19.5 minutes in 2000/01. That's a ratio bettered by only three Premiership defenders.

JOE COLE

Age: 19 Position: Midfield

Years before he even broke into the West Ham first team, the name of Joe Cole was known by football fans around England. Word spread about his extraordinary ball skills when Joe was still in his early teens and he was labelled "the next Gazza". The lad himself prefers to go his own way though. "I never try to copy someone else," says Joe. "I'm my own player."

Every manager in the country was after him – former West Ham manager Harry Redknapp used to joke that the first thing Sir Alex Ferguson said to him on the phone wasn't "Hello", but "How's that boy Cole?"

Now well established in the Hammers' first-team set-up, Cole will be looking to make his mark at international level.

Natural talent: 10/10

Prospects: 10/10

DID YOU KNOW?
In 2000/01 Joe Cole made 55 successful dribbles in Premier League games – only Man United winger Ryan Giggs made more.

KIERON DYER

Age: 22 Position: Midfield

Kieron's talent was nurtured at Ipswich Town and his profile rose dramatically when he joined Newcastle United for £6 million in July 1999. Good performances in his first season caught the eye of then England manager Kevin Keegan and Kieron soon added full international caps to his collection of Under-21 and B team honours.

Although Kieron only weighs 10 stone, his balanced running style makes him hard to shake off the ball and he has the speed to burn past burly defenders. His ability to play in a variety of positions also gives managers valuable options.

In spring he went under the surgeon's knife to cure a painful shin splints problem. England fans will be hoping he returns as good as new.

Natural talent: 8/10

Prospects: 9/10

DID YOU KNOW?
Kieron Dyer had an 81% pass completion rate in 2000/01 making him one of the top ten most accurate Premirship passers.

STEVEN GERRARD

Age: 21 Position: Midfield

Voted the 2001 PFA Young Player of the Year, Steven Gerrard was arguably Liverpool's most important player during their Treble-winning year.

A steely competitor and an excellent tackler, Steven is also a perceptive passer with the ability to unleash fearsome long-range shots.

He made his international debut as a substitute against Ukraine in a pre-Euro 2000 friendly and was impressive in his first half-hour wearing the Three Lions. Only persistent back injuries have limited his England outings since. Despite achieving so much so young, he's not going to dwell on his successes. "Hopefully, I'll be as good as Keane and Vieira next season…," he declared in April, "…if not better!"

Natural talent: 9/10

Prospects: 10/10

DID YOU KNOW?
Steven Gerrard made more passes (1,430) and more tackles (124) than any of his Liverpool team-mates in 2000/01.

ALAN SMITH

Age: 20 Position: Striker

The Leeds star showed his quality in 2000/01 scoring five goals in Leeds run to the Champions League semi-final. His finest moment came in the second phase match against Lazio, when he scored Leeds' winning goal in Rome.

A tenacious player who will fight to win every ball, Alan is also a sharp finisher. The one weakness in his make-up is that his will to win occasionally spills over into aggression. Leeds manager David O'Leary publicly scolded the young striker after he was needlessly sent-off for a late tackle in the final minutes of the Champions League semi-final defeat by Valencia. But Smithy is just 20 years old and he still has plenty of time to get established in the full England side.

Natural talent: 8/10

Prospects: 8/10

DID YOU KNOW?
Hard-working Alan Smith attempted 55 tackles during the 2000/01 Premiership – a tally that can only be bettered by Paolo Di Canio among top-flight strikers.

BEHIND THE SCENES AT ON THE BALL

Every Saturday afternoon, millions of viewers tune in to watch *On The Ball* presented by Gabby Yorath and Barry Venison. So what goes into making this super football show? We went behind-the-scenes to find out...

10.00am

BREAKING NEWS

It's over three hours until showtime, but the *On The Ball* production team are already hard at work in the office. Big news has broken that Sir Alex Ferguson will leave Manchester United completely when he finishes as manager in 2002. This must be included in the show and producer Nick Moody is on the phone to the Head of ITV Sport to discuss how they will handle the issue.

CH-CH-CH-CH-CHANGES!

Production Assistant, Mary Hutchinson, types in the necessary changes to the running order. There will now be a five-minute feature on Sir Alex Ferguson at the top of the show including a video report, a live link to Dave Beckett at White Hart Lane and a studio chat with Barry and Andy.

10.50am

11.00am

LOOKING GOOD

It's time to get ready for rehearsals and everyone moves down from the 19th floor office to the *On The Ball* studio on the first floor. Gabby is the first in the make-up room where Joanne Frye applies a touch of blusher and a dab of lipstick. A natural beauty, Gabby doesn't need much war paint!

12.22pm

DIRECTION FROM THE GALLERY

The rehearsals are a last opportunity to change things that aren't working well. All the presenters have headsets so the production team in the viewing gallery can communicate with them. Here, *On The Ball* Director, Jamie Oakford, is making a point.

12.55pm

BAZ AND ANDY TAKE A BREAK

With the rehearsal successfully completed, Gabby has to stay in the studio to record a couple of voice-overs, but Andy and Barry retire to the Green Room for a swift orange juice...

10.30am GET MOVING, DAVE!

Nick tells reporter Dave Beckett to go down to White Hart Lane where Manchester United are playing their last league game of the season against Spurs. Dave's job will be to do a live interview with former United player Arthur Albiston during the show.

10.40am GABBY, BARRY AND ANDY GET THEIR HEADS TOGETHER...

Presenters Gabby Yorath and Barry Venison grab a quiet corner with guest Andy Townsend to talk about today's show. The schedule includes a feature on the battle for the last Champions League place plus interviews with West Ham starlet, Joe Cole, Charlton boss, Alan Curbishley and Celtic hotshot, Henrik Larsson. Between video clips, Gabby and the lads only have a couple of minutes to talk so they have to plan what they want to say.

10.45am CUT HENRIK!

Executive producer David Moss and Nick Moody explain that they are going to have to drop the Henrik Larsson interview to fit in the story on Sir Alex Ferguson. It's a shame for Gabby who went all the way to Glasgow to interview Larsson a couple of days before, but these things often happen with television shows and she takes it all in her stride.

11.55am IN THE GREEN ROOM

The Green Room is a place where everyone involved in the show can relax, have a cup of tea and a croissant and watch telly. Gabby and Nick are making some final adjustments to her script which Gabby writes herself. "If someone else writes it for you, it doesn't sound natural," she explains.

11.25am MEANWHILE, IN THE LADS' ROOM...

Barry gets prepared in the dressing room he sometimes shares with John Barnes. Sadly, there's no sign of the loud suits he used to wear – nowadays Barry opts for more sober colours. "All those stripes made the TV screen strobe and the producer banned me from wearing them," jokes Baz.

12.05pm "IT'S REHEARSAL TIME, CHAPS..."

Floor Manager Ken has organised everything in the *On The Ball* studio and he calls Gabby, Barry and Andy to come in for rehearsals.

12.15pm GETTING MIKED UP

Andy gets his microphone fitted while Gabby and Barry scribble down some more notes, Then it's time to rehearse the whole show from start to finish.

1.10pm FIVE MINUTES TO GO...

Barry and Andy return to the set for the real thing. Barry looks very happy!!

1.15pm IT'S SHOWTIME!

"Welcome to the final *On The Ball* of the season..." Gabby introduces the show. They're off and running.

1.55pm GROUP HUG

It's the end of another brilliant show and a great series. Before the *On The Ball* set is dismantled for summer, the whole team get together for a group hug. Well done, everyone!

PREMIERSHIP POSERS

The Premiership isn't a sprint, it's a marathon. So test your footie stamina with our top flight quiz!

EYES WITHOUT A FACE
Try and identify Premiership stars from their twinkling eyes!

TOP DIVISION TEASERS

1 Which team who wear red-and-white striped shirts were not awarded a single penalty in the 2000/01 season?

2 Leeds striker Mark Viduka scored more headers in the Premiership than any other player last season. Did he score: a) 6 b) 8 or c) 10?

3 How long did it take substitute Ole Gunnar Solskjaer to score four goals against Nottingham Forest in the 8–1 thrashing of Forest in February 1999: a) 6 minutes b) 11 minutes c) 16 minutes

4 What is the name of Ian Harte's uncle who also plays for Leeds United?

5 True or false – Dwight Yorke has a scar in the shape of Tobago on his back?

6 Southampton striker James Beattie joined the Saints from which club – clue: they were promoted to the Premiership in 2000/01?

7 What nationality is Newcastle midfielder Clarence Acuna?

8 Which goalkeeper conceded 57 goals, more than any other Premiership keeper in the league last season: a) Mart Poom b) Nicky Weaver or c) Matt Clarke

9 Before he went to Anfield, which club did Liverpool midfielder Danny Murphy play for?

10 Which Chelsea midfielder scored 11 goals last season, more than any other Premiership midfielder?

11 Which two players got sent off for violent conduct when Sunderland lost 0–1 to Manchester United at the Stadium Of Light in January 2001?

12 What's the name of Chelsea's lion mascot?

13 Manchester United winger Luke Chadwick once played on loan for which Belgian club?

14 Arsenal and Charlton were involved in the highest scoring match of the 2000/01 Premiership totalling eight goals between them. What was the final score?

15 In which year was veteran Premiership hotshot Teddy Sheringham born?

16 Who was the 2001 PFA Young Player Of The Year?

17 Which team does Prime Minister Tony Blair support?

18 How many goals did the Premiership's top scorer Jimmy Floyd Hasselbaink score in 2000/01?

19 Which Premiership ground hosted England's game against Finland in February 2001?

20 Sunderland manager Peter Reid won the League Championship twice as a player for which club?

SEARCH FOR THE STARS
Can you find these famous names hidden in this alphabet maze. Beware – they can be backwards, forwards, up, down or diagonal!

AMEOBI
BEATTIE
BOKSIC
BRAMBLE

DUBLIN
FLOWERS
FOWLER
HAALAND
HIGGINBOTHAM
HUNT

COLLINS
DACOURT
DALLA BONA

JANSEN
JOHNSON
KEOWN
KILBANE
KINKLADZE
HUGHES
LJUNGBERG
MELCHIOT

NEVILLE
POOM
POWELL
REBROV
REDKNAPP
SAHA
SCHOLES

SHEARER

SINCLAIR
SOUTHGATE
STEWART
STURRIDGE
TAGGART
WOODGATE
YORKE

T	H	R	I	A	L	C	N	I	S	S	E	E	P	P	A	N	K	D	E	R
N	A	L	M	O	T	R	L	W	O	A	R	M	U	B	E	A	T	T	I	E
U	J	B	E	T	A	G	D	O	O	W	E	E	N	I	G	R	E	B	U	A
H	M	L	T	R	J	A	N	S	E	N	A	G	W	E	N	A	B	L	I	K
Y	E	R	B	U	E	G	D	I	R	R	U	T	S	O	E	W	M	O	O	P
E	G	R	E	B	G	N	U	J	L	B	R	T	A	T	L	T	K	E	E	P
S	R	A	P	E	L	B	M	A	R	B	E	E	R	T	G	F	N	E	N	A
L	I	N	O	W	T	V	C	B	A	W	E	K	E	M	I	T	I	L	Y	N
E	H	U	G	H	E	S	O	E	A	S	O	B	E	B	F	H	L	T	T	O
C	H	A	N	C	E	R	E	R	I	A	Y	M	E	O	E	E	B	R	S	B
R	O	E	I	T	O	E	T	A	B	L	E	A	U	E	W	H	U	A	U	A
D	A	K	G	N	O	L	A	T	R	E	E	H	L	O	E	N	D	G	J	L
N	B	R	M	M	T	R	L	A	O	I	R	T	P	B	G	F	P	G	B	L
A	X	O	M	E	L	C	H	I	O	T	E	O	S	Y	X	E	B	A	O	A
L	L	Y	G	R	T	E	R	E	N	E	O	B	I	L	L	A	E	T	K	D
A	M	E	O	B	I	E	W	O	E	S	E	N	O	S	N	H	O	J	S	T
A	R	V	E	I	R	V	T	W	E	L	L	I	V	E	N	A	K	E	I	A
H	V	T	E	A	W	N	O	D	R	A	P	G	O	H	T	S	E	E	C	R
I	E	Z	E	Q	Y	F	O	W	L	E	R	G	L	J	U	N	Y	F	W	A
T	E	H	E	T	A	G	H	T	U	O	S	I	E	S	E	L	O	H	C	S
V	S	E	Z	D	A	L	K	N	I	K	E	H	E	T	R	U	O	C	A	D

Job-sharing with Roy Evans didn't work out.

Houillier has brought in his own men.

Sending out the right messages.

"Nice one, Robbie..."

... You're not bad either, Mikel!"

When Gerard Houllier became Liverpool manager in 1998, he faced the daunting task of recapturing the world-famous Anfield club's former glories. Three years later, he led them to an incredible cup treble. So what are the secrets of the Houllier Revolution?

THE EXPERIENCE

To understand the character of the manager who led Liverpool to the triumphs of 2000/01, you have to look back to his early experiences in football. An English teacher by profession, Gerard Houllier built his reputation as a part-time coach with Le Touquet and Noeux-les-Mines. Officials at professional club Lens were impressed and decided to take him on.

"We could see he was a rigorous, intelligent coach," recalls Louis Plet, the General Secretary of Lens.

But Houillier's lack of a playing career proved to be a problem in gaining the respect of top players. Some dismissed him as a "blackboard coach" and he was the butt of a few jokes when he became Michel Platini's assistant with the French national team. Platini himself would sometimes quip, "Come on, professor. Show us how it's done" (of course, he couldn't).

And when Houllier became the national team manager and they subsequently failed to qualify for the 1994 World Cup finals, the media put all the blame at his door.

Houllier decided that he would no longer let players take liberties with him and became a firmer disciplinarian. He was rewarded for his efforts in 1998 when he helped France to World Cup victory as the team's Technical Director.

THE BACKROOM STAFF

After an ill-fated job-sharing spell with Roy Evans, Houllier took over managerial duties at Liverpool FC in July 1998. He showed his appreciation of Liverpool's glorious history by surrounding himself with heroes from the past.

Assistant manager, Phil Thompson, remembers his first meeting with Houllier well: "We sat and discussed our football beliefs and what we wanted from the game. I was impressed by his passion for the club. He'd lived here before as a young man so he had a feeling for the city."

Thompson's fiery nature on the touchline is in sharp contrast to Houllier's more measured approach, but they have proved to be a great combination.

Meanwhile, Steve Heighway, a winger during Liverpool's golden era two decades ago, looks after the Youth Academy that has produced superb players such as Steven Gerrard.

"The good thing about the staff here is that they keep your feet on the ground," says Gerrard. "They've been there and won most of the trophies we're playing for. When they are telling you something, you've got to listen."

THE ATTITUDE

Don't be fooled by his Inspector Clouseau looks, Houllier is nobody's fool. "He is strong and hard," insists his assistant Phil Thompson. "If there is

"He is strong and hard. Gerard goes about his business quietly, but never, ever, cross him."

discipline to be handed out, they don't come harder than Gerard Houllier. He reminds me of Joe Fagan (legendary Liverpool coach and manager). He goes about his business quietly, but never, ever, cross him."

That view is backed up by the players. "The training is great and he makes sure we enjoy ourselves," says club captain Jamie Redknapp. "But he's a real perfectionist. If we're having a team talk and he sees someone isn't concentrating, he's on to them right away."

And the fact that the "Spice Boys" image Liverpool players had in the mid-1990s has gone now is down to Houllier's influence. His advice to Steven Gerrard is simply:

"The next ten years can be the best of Steven's life, but he has to live for the job', he warns. "If his mates want to go to a nightclub, let them. By the time Steven has finished he can buy his own."

LUTION

THE RIGHT BLEND

Houllier has assembled a strong and balanced squad. He's taken a sprinkling of homegrown youngsters (Danny Murphy, Robbie Fowler, Steven Gerrard...), added some top foreign players (Sami Hyppia, Dietmar Hamann and Jari Litmanen...) and thrown in a couple of big-money signings (Emile Heskey, Nicky Barmby...) for good measure.

Don't forget the dash of experience either because 36-year-old midfielder Gary McAllister was a revelation in Liverpool's UEFA Cup-winning run.

"He wants us to play good passing football and that's how I like to see the game played as well," says McAllister. "Perhaps he wanted an old head in the middle of the park to offer some advice and guidance. That's what I try to do. If I can help the younger guys to improve just one percent that'll do for me."

Now the only remaining question is whether Houllier has the right stuff to challenge Manchester United's Premiership dominance.

GERARD HOULLIER
A MANAGERS LIFE

1973-76	Le Touquet
1976-82	Noeux-les-Mines
1982-85	Lens
1985-88	Paris St. Germain
	Won French Championship in 1986
1988-92	France (Assistant)
1992-93	France
1993-98	France (Technical Director)
	Won World Cup in 1998
1998-	Liverpool
	Won Worthington Cup, FA Cup and UEFA Cup in 2001

HARD MEN

ROY KEANE v ROBBIE SAVAGE

With his lavish blond locks and designer label tattoo, you could be mistaken for thinking that Robbie Savage is a bit of a lightweight. Put him on a football pitch though, and the Leicester City star turns into a competitive little so-and-so. But he can't quite deal with the fearsome Man United captain who was an unbeaten amateur boxer in his youth. Keano's shaven head and scary temper prove too much and the Savage is savaged.

Result: Keano wins by a haircut.

DENNIS WISE v PAUL INCE

Despite his small stature, Dennis the Menace could probably start a barney in a monastery. But with Middlesbrough firebrand Paul "The Guv'nor" Ince in the opposite corner he doesn't have to go looking for trouble. Wisey's tactic of pinching opponents' thighs is thwarted by wearing boxing gloves and Incey, who has been trained by his cousin, the former middleweight champion of the world Nigel "Dark Destroyer" Benn, takes full advantage.

Result: Incey chops down the Chelsea captain.

The Premiership is no place for the faint-hearted. There's some tough cookies roaming the pitches who aren't afraid to get stuck in where it hurts as they battle for supremacy. Just for fun, we pitted eight of the hardest characters against each other in a fantasy fight tournament. Who will be the last man standing? If you are squeamish, please turn the page now!

PATRICK VIEIRA v TIM SHERWOOD

This North London derby match-up is a thrilling affair. Shaggy-haired Sherwood is an wily old campaigner who knows all the tricks and he isn't intimidated by the lanky Frenchman. But although Vieira has cut down on the bookings in recent times, he's lost none of his will to win, and after a bloody contest, the Gunner shoots down Sherwood to claim a place in the semi-final.

Result: Patrick wins on points after bruising battle.

DAVID BATTY v STUART PEARCE

These two veterans have both experienced the pain of missing penalties in World Cup shoot-outs… and they've both dished out a lot of painful tackles in their time. Sturdy Yorkshireman Bats has ruled the Leeds midfield for years while Pearcey scares the wits out of opposing wingers with his psycho stare and humungous thighs. This really is a close call, but while Bats is arguing with fight fan Graeme Le Saux, 39-year-old Psycho kicks him into the stand to win by TKO.

Result: Psycho batters Batty into submission.

ROY KEANE v PAUL INCE

They used to play together in the heart of Manchester United's midfield, but there's no room for sentiment as the two hard men get stuck into each other. Big-punching Incey piles up an early points advantage, but Keano rekindles the magic of United's 1999 European Cup semi-final win over Juventus, producing a miraculous comeback to win by late KO.

Result: Keano shows the Guv'nor who's boss.

PATRICK VIEIRA v STUART PEARCE

The gangling Frenchman ties Psycho up in knots in the early stages, but Pearcey shows the Bulldog spirit to fight his way back into the contest. In the end, with neither man backing down, the ref intervenes and offers each man one free punch at their foe. Pearcey has first go, but haunted by flashbacks to his 1990 World Cup semi-final nightmare, he misses and Vieira knocks out the last remaining Englishman from the tournament.

Result: Pat pulverises Pearcey.

ROY KEANE v PATRICK VIEIRA

Blood, guts and gore… that's what every footie fight fan expects when Roy Keane goes head to head with Arsenal's midfield general. But after five suitably fierce rounds, Keano grabs the ringside announcer's microphone and announces: "Fighting is no way to solve our problems. C'mon, Pat, let's go and grab a coffee and talk it over." Pat agrees, hugging his former rival and saying: "Roy's right, let's give peace a chance. Bless you all."

Result: Erm, world peace?

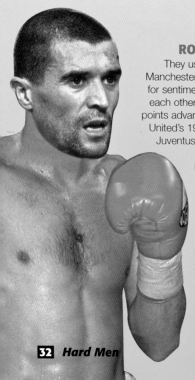

MAGIC MOMENTS

> "
>
> My favourite moment of last season was Gary McAllister's superb free-kick against Everton in the Merseyside derby. I've played in those derbies myself and this one brought memories flooding back to me. It was one of those games that had everything – two fiercely competitive teams, a lot of goals, a bit of controversy and some great moments of skill. None better than Gary's long-range strike that gave the visitors a 3–2 victory in stoppage time. Pure drama – which is what football's all about.
>
> "

EURO QUEST

LEEDS UNITED

Leeds proved to be the most successful English team in the Champions League last year, but no-one was predicting they would reach the semi-finals when they were thrashed 4–0 by mighty Barcelona in their opening game. Weakened by injuries, David O'Leary's team had no answer as goals by Patrick Kluivert (two), Rivaldo and Frank De Boer gave them a harsh introduction to top-class European football.

But O'Leary's young side proved their powers of recovery by grabbing an amazing 1–0 win in their next match against Italian giants AC Milan. In the 89th minute on a rainy night at Elland Road, Milan keeper Didi allowed a Lee Bowyer shot to slip through his fingers and gift Leeds the points.

Leeds then pulverised Turkish club Besiktas 6–0 (amazingly, Besiktas had beaten Barcelona 3–0 the previous week) and this fantastic result lifted Leeds to the top of Group H after three games. When Barcelona visited Elland Road in October, a fifth-minute goal by Lee Bowyer put Leeds 1–0 up before Rivaldo sneaked one for

Semi-final agony for Leeds...

Barça in the fourth minute of stoppage time. Leeds were not to be denied a place in the second phase, though, and a gritty 1–1 draw against group winners AC Milan secured their qualification.

Leeds then faced the awesome challenge of playing European champions Real Madrid and moneybags Italian team Lazio in phase two. Real's class and experience were too much for

Leeds in the opening game. Fernando Hierro and Raul both netted goals in a dazzling three-minute second-half spell to secure a 2–0 win.

Leeds' players never say die though and a marvellous 1–0 away win against Lazio put them back on course for the last eight. Alan Smith's winning goal with ten minutes remaining after a nonchalant back-flick by strike partner Mark Viduka was just reward for a great team performance. Lazio never recovered from this shock and two wins for Leeds against Anderlecht all but secured their quarter-final slot.

By spring, after a season of injury worries, David O'Leary had many of his key players, like Harry Kewell and David Batty, playing regularly again. So a quarter-final against Spanish skillsters Deportivo La Coruna held no fears for them. Ian Harte's trademark free-kick after 26 minutes set Leeds on the way to a superb 3–0 first-leg win that effectively guaranteed their presence in the last four.

They faced 2000 Champions League finalists Valencia in the semi-final. Leeds dominated the second-half of the first match at Elland Road, with Dominic Matteo having a header punched off the line by Valencia keeper Santiago Canizares and Lee Bowyer hitting the crossbar in the 70th minute. But the match ended 0–0, and Valencia turned up the heat in Spain to record a comprehensive 3–0 win. Leeds' rollercoaster journey had come to an end, but what a great ride!

CHAMPIONS LEAGUE 2000/01: LEEDS UNITED RESULTS

FIRST PHASE

Date	Opponents	Score	Leeds goalscorers/mins
13 Sep	Barcelona (a)	lost 0–4	
19 Sep	AC Milan (h)	won 1–0	Bowyer 89
26 Sep	Besiktas (h)	won 6–0	Bowyer 7, 90; Viduka 12; Matteo 22; Bakke 65; Huckerby 90
18 Oct	Besiktas (a)	drew 0–0	
24 Oct	Barcelona (h)	drew 1–1	Bowyer 5
8 Nov	AC Milan (a)	drew 1–1	Matteo 45

GROUP H FINAL TABLE

	P	W	D	L	F	A	Pts
1 AC Milan	6	3	2	1	12	6	11
2 Leeds United	6	2	3	1	9	6	9
3 Barcelona	6	2	2	2	13	9	8
4 Besiktas	6	1	1	4	4	17	4

SECOND PHASE

Date	Opponents	Score	Leeds goalscorers/mins
22 Nov	Real Madrid (h)	lost 0–2	
5 Dec	Lazio (a)	won 1–0	Smith 80
13 Feb	Anderlecht (h)	won 2–1	Harte 74, Bowyer 87
21 Feb	Anderlecht (a)	won 4–1	Smith 13, 38; Viduka 34; Harte 81
6 Mar	Real Madrid (a)	lost 2–3	Smith 6; Viduka 54
14 Mar	Lazio (h)	drew 3–3	Bowyer 28, Wilcox 43; Viduka 62

GROUP D FINAL TABLE

	P	W	D	L	F	A	Pts
1 Real Madrid	6	4	1	1	14	9	13
2 Leeds United	6	3	1	2	12	10	10
3 Anderlecht	6	2	0	4	7	12	6
4 Lazio	6	1	2	3	9	11	5

QUARTER-FINAL

Date	Opponent	Score	Leeds goalscorers/mins
4 Apr	Deportivo La Coruna (h)	won 3–0	Harte 26; Smith 51; Ferdinand 66
17 Apr	Deportivo La Coruna (a)	lost 0–2	Leeds United win 3–2 on aggregate

SEMI-FINAL

Date	Opponent	Score	Leeds goalscorers/mins
2 May	Valencia (h)	drew 0–0	
8 May	Valencia (a)	lost 0–3	
Leeds United lose 0–3 on aggregate			

Leeds players had a never-say-die attitude in Europe.

In 2000/01, English clubs produced their best showing in European competition for many years. The three Premiership representatives in the Champions League – Manchester United, Arsenal and Leeds United – all battled through to the knock-out phase of the tournament. And just to underline the strength of our league football, resurgent Liverpool also produced a great run to win the Uefa Cup. Let's look back at an exciting season for the Big Four in Europe…

CHAMPIONS LEAGUE 2000/01: ARSENAL RESULTS

FIRST PHASE

Date	Opponents	Score	Arsenal goalscorers/mins
12 Sep	Sparta Praha (a)	won 1–0	Silvinho 33
20 Sep	Shakhtar Donetsk (h)	won 3–2	Wiltord 45; Keown 85, 90
27 Sep	Lazio (h)	won 2–0	Ljungberg 43, 56
17 Oct	Lazio (a)	drew 1–1	Pires 88
25 Oct	Sparta Praha (h)	won 4–2	Parlour 5, Lauren 8, Dixon 35, Kanu 51
7 Nov	Shakhtar Donetsk (a)	lost 0–3	

GROUP B FINAL TABLE

	P	W	D	L	F	A	Pts
1 Arsenal	6	4	1	1	11	8	13
2 Lazio	6	4	1	1	13	4	13
3 Shakhtar Donetsk	6	2	0	4	10	15	6
4 Sparta Praha	6	1	0	5	6	13	3

SECOND PHASE

Date	Opponents	Score	Arsenal goalscorers/mins
22 Nov	Spartak Moscow (a)	lost 1–4	Silvinho 2
5 Dec	Bayern Munich (h)	drew 2–2	Henry 4, Kanu 55
13 Feb	Lyon (a)	won 1–0	Henry 59
21 Feb	Lyon (h)	drew 1–1	Bergkamp 33
6 Mar	Spartak Moscow (h)	won 1–0	Henry 82
14 Mar	Bayern Munich (h)	lost 0–1	

GROUP C FINAL TABLE

	P	W	D	L	F	A	Pts
1 Bayern Munich	6	4	1	1	8	5	13
2 Arsenal	6	2	2	2	6	8	8
3 Lyon	6	2	2	2	8	4	8
4 Spartak Moscow	6	1	1	4	5	10	4

QUARTER FINAL

Date	Opponent	Score	Arsenal goalscorers/mins
4 Apr	Valencia (h)	won 2–1	Henry 58
17 Apr	Valencia (a)	lost 0–1	Parlour 60

Aggregate score 2–2 – Arsenal lose on away goals

ARSENAL

In recent years, Arsenal's main problem in Europe has been their form in home matches which they played at Wembley. Having won just two of six Champions League games under the Twin Towers, European football came back to Highbury in 2000/01. The wisdom of this decision was shown in the Gunners' first home tie of the season against Shakhtar Donetsk. After falling 2–0 behind, the Highbury faithful roared Arsenal on to a miraculous 3–2 victory with defender Martin Keown scoring two goals in the last five minutes.

Arsenal followed up with a 2–0 home win over Lazio's star-studded team – Swedish midfielder Freddie Ljungberg grabbed the vital goals either side of half time. Robert Pires's 88th-minute equaliser in Rome three weeks later meant it had taken the Gunners just four games to blast their way into phase two with ten points from four games. And for good measure, a 4–2 victory over Sparta Praha (that was three wins out of three at Highbury) ensured they'd win the group, too.

The second phase proved to be much more difficult for the Gunners. Wenger's boys got off to a dreadful start at the Luzhniki Stadium in Moscow, losing 4–1 to Russian champions Spartak Moscow. In artic conditions, Arsenal took

The second phase proved to be much trickier for the Gunners.

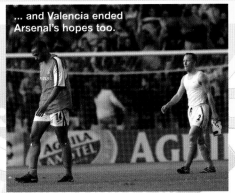

… and Valencia ended Arsenal's hopes too.

the lead after just 76 seconds through Silvinho, but two goals by Spartak's Brazilian striker, Marcao, and late strikes by Robson and Egor Titov made sure it was a miserable journey home for the Arsenal squad.

A fortnight later, Bayern Munich earned a 2–2 draw at Highbury leaving Arsenal still needing points. Two crucial goals by French hotshot Thierry Henry secured them. The first was the carefully-placed header from Ashley Cole's cross to beat Olympique Lyonnais in Lyon. Then in their penultimate Group C match at home to Spartak Moscow, Henry's 82nd-minute header gave Arsenal three more crucial points and put them on the brink of qualification. A 0–1 away loss to group winners Bayern Munich saw Arsenal finish level on points with Lyon, but Arsenal went through because of better results against the French club.

In the quarter-final, Arsenal faced Valencia. Another goal from Henry and a magnificent long-range strike by Ray Parlour gave Arsenal a 2–1 lead going into the second leg. Sadly, a fine twisting header by Valencia striker John Carew with just 15 minutes remaining at the Mestalla Stadium meant that Valencia won on away goals and Arsene Wenger's European dream was over.

CHAMPIONS LEAGUE 2000/01: MANCHESTER UNITED RESULTS

FIRST PHASE

Date	Opponents	Score	United goalscorers/mins
13 Sep	Anderlecht (h)	won 5–1	Cole 15, 50, 72; Irwin 32; Sheringham 42
19 Sep	Dynamo Kiev (a)	drew 0–0	
26 Sep	PSV Eindhoven (a)	lost 1–3	Scholes 3
18 Oct	PSV Eindhoven (h)	won 3–1	Sheringham 8; Scholes 82; Yorke 87
24 Oct	Anderlecht (a)	lost 1–2	Irwin pen 36
8 Nov	Dynamo Kiev (h)	won 1–0	Sheringham 18

GROUP G FINAL TABLE

	P	W	D	L	F	A	Pts
1 Anderlecht	6	4	0	2	11	14	12
2 Manchester United	6	3	1	2	11	7	10
3 PSV Eindhoven	6	3	0	3	9	9	9
4 Dynamo Kiev	6	1	1	4	7	8	4

SECOND PHASE

Date	Opponents	Score	United goalscorers/mins
21 Nov	Panathanaikos (h)	won 3–1	Sheringham 48; Scholes 81, 90
6 Dec	Sturm Graz (a)	won 2–0	Scholes 18; Giggs 89
14 Feb	Valencia (a)	drew 0–0	
20 Feb	Valencia (h)	drew 1–1	Cole 12
7 Mar	Panathanaikos (a)	drew 1–1	Scholes 90
13 Mar	Sturm Graz (h)	won 3–0	Butt 5; Sheringham 20; Keane 86

GROUP A FINAL TABLE

	P	W	D	L	F	A	Pts
1 Valencia	6	3	3	0	10	2	12
2 Manchester United	6	3	3	0	10	3	12
3 Sturm Graz	6	2	0	4	4	13	6
4 Panathanaikos	6	0	2	4	4	10	2

QUARTER-FINAL

Date	Opponent	Score	United goalscorers/mins
3 Apr	Bayern Munich (h)	lost 0–1	
18 Apr	Bayern Munich (a)	lost 1–2	Giggs 49

Mancheser United lose 1–3 on aggregate

MANCHESTER UNITED

The 1999 European champions never quite got into gear during the 2000/01 tournament. It appeared to be business as usual as the Red machine crushed Anderlecht in their first fixture. Hotshot Andy Cole grabbed a brilliant hat-trick that took his career tally in Champions League matches to 17, making him the club's all-time top scorer in European Cup competition.

But after such a bright start, United's away form let them down, losing two and drawing one of their three first phase matches on foreign soil. United faced the real prospect of elimination unless they could beat Dynamo Kiev in their final group game at Old Trafford. United took the lead in the 18th minute through Teddy Sheringham. With five minutes to go, disaster almost struck. Kiev broke sharply down the right wing and the ball was cut back to substitute George Demetradze who somehow missed from six yards out and United lived to fight another day.

Roy Keane was highly critical of United's fans after the match, claiming they were more worried about eating prawn sandwiches than supporting the team. His words had an effect and the atmosphere was crackling for the Reds opening match in the second phase against Panathanaikos. The players responded with a good performance and a 3–1 win courtesy of second-half goals by Teddy Sheringham and Paul Scholes (two).

A comfortable 2–0 win against Sturm Graz at the Arnold Schwarzenegger Stadium left Sir Alex Ferguson's men sitting pretty at the top of Group A before the winter break.

Ultimately, United's away form let them down...

However, when play resumed in February, United lost their way, drawing three matches in a row and scoring just two goals in the process. Again, United found themselves in a situation where they had to win the last group game to qualify. Fortunately, it was a home match against Sturm Graz, a team United had beaten three times out of three in the past two seasons. A rocket shot by Nicky Butt after five minutes set the Reds on the way to victory and a quarter-final tie against Bayern Munich.

Bayern players were desperate to avenge their defeat by United in the 1999 final and they made a great start by winning the first leg at Old Trafford 1–0 with a late goal by substitute Paulo Sergio. Thousands of United fans travelled to the Olympic Stadium in Munich knowing that nothing less than victory would do. But any realistic hopes of a win were extinguished when Brazilian striker Elber and Mehmet Scholl made the score 3–0 on aggregate before half-time. United attacked with gusto in the second-half and Ryan Giggs pulled a goal back with a neat lob, but it was too little too late. The Red Devils were out.

Despite captain Keane's best efforts, United were found wanting in Europe.

LIVERPOOL
UEFA CUP CHAMPS!

Liverpool's triumphant UEFA Cup campaign started in low-key style with an unimpressive 1–0 aggregate win over Romanian side Rapid Bucharest. Houllier's men performed similarly poorly in the second round first leg at Anfield against Czech Cup winners Slovan Liberec. An 87th-minute strike by Emile Heskey gave 'Pool a narrow advantage going into the away leg, but goals from Heskey, Nicky Barmby and Michael Owen in Liberec secured their passage through to the next round.

After another 4–2 aggregate win, against Olympiakos, Liverpool faced Italian Serie A leaders Roma in the fourth round. The first leg was played at the Olympic Stadium in Rome where Liverpool had previously won two

European Cup finals (in 1977 and 1984). It proved a happy hunting ground again and two fantastic strikes by Michael Owen earned 'Pool victory. Roma fought back bravely in the return match, winning 1–0, but Liverpool were through to the quarter-final where they took on Porto.

After a dour goalless draw in Portugal, two goals in five first-half minutes by Danny Murphy and Michael Owen earned Liverpool a semi-final clash with Spanish giants Barcelona. Again, Liverpool put up a first-leg defensive blockade to earn a goalless draw in front of a 90,000 crowd at the Nou Camp. Back at Anfield, a moment of madness by Dutch star Patrick Kluivert, who handled the ball as he rose to make a defensive header, gifted Liverpool a crucial penalty. Gary

McAllister cooly slotted home the 44th-minute spot-kick to win the tie.

36-year old McAllister was the hero again in the thrilling 5–4 final win against plucky Spanish minnows Alaves in Dortmund. Man-of-the-match McAllister scored one and set up three goals including the crucial golden goal. It was his teasing free-kick that flicked off Alaves defender Delfi Geli Roura's head into the net in the 117th minute to clinch Liverpool's first European trophy win for 17 years and a remarkable cup treble. Afterwards, joyous McAllister gushed: "It's amazing, I can't believe it. It's still not sunk in, but I know that winning a cup treble is a great achievement. It will take me all summer to recover from this one!"

UEFA Cup 2000/01: LIVERPOOL RESULTS

ROUND ONE

v Rapid Bucharest: won 1–0 aggregate

14 Sep	(a) won 1–0	Barmby 29
28 Sep	(h) drew 0–0	

ROUND TWO

v Slovan Liberec: won 4–2 aggregate

26 Oct (h)	won 1–0	Heskey 87
9 Nov (a)	won 3–2	Barmby 32; Heskey 76; Owen 82

ROUND THREE

v Olympiakos Piraeus: won 4–2 aggregate

23 Nov (a)	drew 2–2	Barmby 38; Gerrard 67;
7 Dec (h)	won 2–0	Heskey 26; Barmby 60

ROUND FOUR

v AS Roma: won 2–1 aggregate

15 Feb (a)	won 2–0	Owen 46, 72
22 Feb (h)	lost 0–1	

QUARTER-FINAL

v Porto: won 2–0 aggregate

8 Mar (a)	drew 0–0	
15 Mar (h)	won 2–0	Murphy 33; Owen 35

SEMI-FINAL

v Barcelona: won 1–0 aggregate

5 April (a)	drew 0–0	
19 April (h)	won 1–0	McAllister pen 45

FINAL

v Alaves 16 May won 5–4
(Westfalen Stadium, Dortmund)
Liverpool win on golden goal

Babbel 4; Gerrard 16; McAllister pen 44; Fowler 73; Geli o.g. 117

UEFA Cup 2000/01: CHELSEA

ROUND ONE

v FC St Gallen: lost 1–2 agg

14 Sep (h)	won 1–0	Panucci 24
28 Sep (h)	lost 0–2	
Chelsea lose 1–2 aggregate		

UEFA Cup 2000/01: LEICESTER CITY

ROUND ONE

v Crvena Zvezda

14 Sep (h)	drew 1–1	Taggart 43
28 Sep (a)	lost 1–3	Izzet 42
Leicester City lose 2–4 aggregate		

The UEFA Cup triumph was the Reds' first Euro win for 17 years.

Jimmy Floyd
Hasselbaink

TAKING THE MIC!

"NAME ON THE TROPHY!" No-one watching the 1999 European Cup Final on telly will forget Clive Tyldesley's immortal words when Ole Gunnar Solskjaer scored Manchester United's equaliser against Bayern Munich in Barcelona. Here, ITV's premier commentator talks about why he decided to take the mic, recalls some of his funniest moments and explains the pleasures of working with Big Ron!

Youthful prowess
"I always wanted to be a football commentator. I don't think I'm the only child who's ever kicked a ball round in his back garden and commentated to himself! And when I was 12, my Mum entered me for a commentators' competition on the BBC – it was open to adults and Ian St John came second. I got a polite letter back saying, 'Well done, son.'"

First TV commentary
"It was quite a famous Manchester derby match at Maine Road on 23 September 1989. City won 5–1 – how times have changed!

"With only a few minutes played there was a crowd disturbance and the referee took the players off the field. I thought, 'Oh great, I've waited all my life to do this job, and this match is going to last eight minutes!' Thankfully, the players did re-appear!"

Big Ron
"Working with Ron is a pleasure. We get on really well. When you are at a tournament and you are away from home for five or six weeks, he's great to have around. Every morning, he's got a smile on his face and I've never heard him moan about

anything. He's great company because if he's not telling you a story, he's asking you a quiz question or singing a song!

"My favourite Ron story proves the adage that you can never get the last word with him. During an Italy game in the1998 World Cup, Ron suddenly said, "Isn't the goalkeeper Peruzzi the one who got into trouble for posing naked in a women's magazine?"

I replied: "Ron, I've no idea. I don't buy those kind of magazines!"

There was a pause and then he quipped, "It was you that lent it to me!"

Best line of commentary
"A lot of things that I said at the conclusion of the 1999 Champions League Final have been repeated to me since. You know, 'They must score, they always score' etc... This might sound weird, but if there's any part of that commentary of which I was particularly pleased, it was the fact that after both Manchester United goals, I shut up for seven or eight seconds! There's a temptation to shout and scream at times like that, but there's no point because viewers are shouting and screaming themselves!"

Most embarrassing moment
"I was a stand-by commentator for ITV at their London studios during the 1986 World Cup in Mexico. An hour before the opening game of the tournament they had lost sound from the commentary team in Mexico! ITV then had a choice between having this rookie (me) on for his first ever TV commentary or asking Brian Moore who was hosting the show to do it. Quite rightly, they chose Brian.

"So I went to a little studio and did a demo commentary instead for practice. At half-time, the score was 1–1... or so I thought. A guy came in and said:

'Just one thing Clive, You're saying 1–1... in the studio, they're saying it's 1–0.'

"It turned out a goal had been incorrectly disallowed for offside, but I hadn't noticed!

"Luckily, that commentary wasn't aired! The next day, the ITV editor was very decent about it, but he said that if I wanted to go home, I could! And I didn't get asked to work for ITV again for another three years!"

Worst commentary position
"I was working for the BBC at the 1994 World Cup in USA. My first game was at the Pasadena Rose Bowl that staged the final. It involved Cameroon and I was very unfamiliar with their players so I went to three of their training sessions leading up to the game. I got to the stadium on the day and found my commentary position – well, I might as well have been in the Goodyear blimp! I'd gone to all this trouble to identify these players beforehand and when they ran out, they were like dots. We were miles away!"

THE FALL & RISE OF
THE TRACTOR

Ipswich Town produced a remarkable performance to qualify for the UEFA Cup in their first year back in the Premiership. The Tractor Boys proved that talent and team spirit are just as important as mega-bucks transfer fees. But success hasn't come easily, as you'll find out when you jump aboard Manager of the Year George Burley's tractor and take a bumpy ride through Ipswich Town FC's history...

DECEMBER 1994

George Burley is appointed manager of Ipswich Town FC. The Blues had lost 13 of their first 20 Premiership matches by that time, but Burley makes a good start, leading Ipswich to a 1–0 away win against Liverpool in his fifth game in charge...

MARCH 1995

... but it doesn't last. A shocking 0–9 reverse at Old Trafford by champions Manchester United is the second loss in a run of eight successive defeats during which time Ipswich concede 23 goals and score, erm, zero!

JANUARY 1996

Ipswich Town turn FA Cup giantkillers, beating Premiership champs Blackburn Rovers 1–0 in an FA Cup third round replay. Young Richard Wright plays brilliantly in goal to deny Shearer and co.

JULY 1997

Midfielder Matty Holland signs for £800,000 from Bournemouth. It will prove a great buy. Incredibly, by the end of 2000/01, Holland had played more than 220 consecutive games for Ipswich

DECEMBER 1996/JANUARY 1997

The youth policy is starting to kick in... Teenager Kieron Dyer makes his debut as sub against Crystal Palace on December 26. A month later, Richard Wright replaces Craig Forrest as Burley's first-choice goalkeeper.

JUNE 1995

Board member David Sheepshanks becomes Ipswich Town's chairman. He and Burley immediately devise a five-year plan to get the club back on top again.

NOVEMBER 1997

Ipswich make an appalling start to the season and by the 9 November they are 21st out of 22 in Division One. The only bright spot is the signing of striker David Johnson from Bury.

MAY 1996

Another disappointment as the Blues just miss out on a promotion play-off place, finishing seventh in Division One a point behind Charlton Athletic.

MAY 1995

Burley's ageing team finish bottom of the Premiership and are relegated to Division One.

MAY 1997

Ipswich make the play-offs but agonisingly lose on away goals to Sheffield United. A 77th-minute goal by United's Andy Walker in the second leg levels the score at 3–3 on aggregate to kill off Blues' hopes.

BOYS

MAY 2001

The Tractor Boys take the Premiership by storm! Hotshot Marcus Stewart scores a total of 19 Premiership goals and the club finish fifth in the Premiership to earn a UEFA Cup place for 2001/02. Well done, lads!

MAY 2000

At last! Ipswich claim a Premiership place. After just missing out on automatic promotion again, they defeat old rivals Bolton 7–3 on aggregate in the semi-final and Barnsley 4–2 in the final.

18

11

DECEMBER 1998

14

Yet another promising youngster, 17-year-old defender Titus Bramble makes his first-team debut against Sheffield United.

FEBRUARY 2000

Marcus Stewart signs for Ipswich. He makes an immediate impression scoring on his debut away to Barnsley and then on his home debut against former club Huddersfield.

17

MAY 1998

David Johnson scores 20 goals in 31 games to catapult Ipswich into the play-offs…

13

JULY 1998

George Burley appoints Stewart Houston as his assistant and Ipswich make a good start to the 1998/99 season in Division One. Young stars Kieron Dyer and Richard Wright are rewarded for their good form with call-ups to the full England squad.

AUGUST 1999

Kieron Dyer is sold to Newcastle in summer… but the £6 million helps to finance the signings of Jermaine Wright, Mike Salmon and John McGreal.

16

MAY 1999

Three unexpected defeats in their last five league matches cost Ipswich automatic promotion. Their dramatic play-off semi-final against Bolton ends 4–4 on aggregate and again Ipswich lose out on the away goals rule.

15

12

MAY 1998

… but sadly they run out of steam and lose 0–2 on aggregate to Charlton in the play-off semi-finals.

He may look like a character from a Robbie Williams video, but he's actually the identikit Premiership footballer. The perfect blend of brain and brawn, skill and speed, he'd give any opponent nightmares!

BRAIN Teddy Sheringham

The thinking man's footballer, Teddy is a yard quicker in his head than other players and his intelligence allows him to find space and time in the most frenetic of matches.

EYES Gary McAllister

36-year-old midfielder Gary was a sensation in Liverpool's cup Treble-winning season. This wily veteran has the vision and passing ability to unlock the best defences in the business.

NOSE Robbie Fowler

The England forward has always had a nose for goal. A natural born finisher, his striking instinct would benefit any top-class team.

RIGHT ARM Roy Keane

In the heat of a midfield battle, there's no-one you'd rather have in your side than the fearsome Manchester United captain. Won't be afraid to use strong-arm tactics if required.

CHEST Alan Shearer

No-one holds the ball up better than the Newcastle and England striker legend. Fire a ball as hard as you like at Big Al and he'll cushion it on his chest to bring it under instant control.

RIGHT LEG Thierry Henry

Built like an Olympic sprinter, Arsenal's World Cup-winning striker has the acceleration to leave any defender trailing in his wake. The perfect man to break down the offside trap.

RIGHT FOOT David Beckham

The best crosser of a ball in the world, Beckham's right-foot is a lethal weapon whether in open play or deadball situations. With Becks' right foot, our cyber-star will be simply irresistible.

FOREHEAD Niall Quinn

Opposition defenders think they must have run over a Black Cat when they go up for a header against the giant Sunderland striker. Niall heads in crosses few others can hope to reach.

MOUTH Paolo Di Canio

No-one is safe when West Ham's temperamental Italian genius opens his mouth – opponents, fans, managers, team-mates, even himself... but he sure is entertaining!

LEFT ARM Martin Keown

The tenacious Arsenal and England defender will fight to win every ball for his team. A powerful man with the wing span of an eagle, his left arm will ward off predatory tacklers.

BUM Patrik Berger

Something for the laydeez! Patrik Berger is admired by many fans for his ball skills, but there are certainly a few girls out there who have taken a shine to his, er, other attributes!

LEFT LEG Ryan Giggs

The jet-heeled Manchester United and Wales winger has been thrilling Premiership crowds for over a decade now. His left leg is one of the most valuable in world football.

LEFT FOOT Harry Kewell

This young Australian has magic in his left foot. When he gets the ball, he's capable of dribbling past one, two, three defenders at a time. Harry packs a fair old shot, too.

FOOTBALL FUNNIES

Football is a funny old game... just check out these cheeky Premiership rib-ticklers!

Playing in goal for England is a high-pressure job. Just one mistake can cost a defeat so only a special type of character can cope. Here, ITV's resident goalkeeping expert, Bob Wilson, gives his views on the qualities required to wear England's number 1 jersey and the stoppers hoping to guard the onion bag for Sven at World Cup 2002…

THE SEAMAN STANDARD

"David Seaman is still England's top goalkeeper. He has so many attributes… knowledge, experience, presence, consistency and he's totally unflappable.

"David is absolutely huge – six foot four inches tall and broad. People don't realise how big he is until they meet him. Whenever I introduce Dave to anybody, the first thing they say is, 'I never realised you were so big!' His sheer size means he gets to shots that others don't and he's amazingly agile for a man of his size.

"The great advantage David Seaman has over others is his consistency. In ten seasons at Arsenal, he's been a winner six times and a runner-up six times in major competitions at home and in Europe. No English goalkeeper can come near to challenging his consistency at the highest level.

"David's only problem is that this country is the worst in the world for putting people on a pedestal and then knocking them off. People keep saying he's too old, yet Italian legend Dino Zoff won the World Cup at the age of 40; Pat Jennings played at the top-level until he was 41; and Peter Shilton was the best goalkeeper in the 1990 World Cup tournament at the tender age of 40! People want things to move on too quickly and it'll only be when goalkeepers like David Seaman retire (he's 38 now) that they will appreciate how good they were.

"When Sven-Goran Eriksson became England boss, he admitted he didn't know much about goalkeeping,and took the advice of experienced coaches. They all told him the same thing – Seaman is the main man."

THE CHALLENGERS

"There are some very good challengers now. I'm a big fan of David James. Like Seaman, his size makes him very intimidating for opposing forwards and he has amazing agility for his size. He has just about the perfect body shape for a goalkeeper… and, indeed, to be a model as he's shown in the past!

"What he's got going against him is that he's made costly errors in big matches. In the two FA Cup finals, he's played absolutely supremely except for two errors – one for Liverpool against United in 1996 when Eric Cantona scored and also for Aston Villa against Chelsea in 2000 which allowed Di Matteo to score – he got punished for both.

"That stigma has stayed with him and he'll

"No English keeper has come near to Seaman's consistency"

have to be very strong-minded. Considering all the attributes he has, David James should have been a stronger challenger earlier.

"Nigel Martyn is also a fine goalkeeper. He has suffered from having to be Number Two to David when he was in his prime. He's not had a chance, but not because of anything he's done wrong."

THE NEXT GENERATION

"Of the young prospects, I rate Richard Wright particularly highly. In 2000/01, he proved what an outstanding young goalkeeper he is. He is, without doubt, a potential England goalkeeper of the future. Ideally, you'd want him to be a bit taller and have a couple of inches more reach. When you are smaller, you need an extra bounce of the feet to cover the goal, but like Bruce Grobbelaar, Richard is amazingly alert and his footwork is incredible.

"At Leeds, Paul Robinson is now pushing Nigel Martyn very hard in the same way that Peter Shilton once pressed Gordon Banks when he burst

on the scene at Leicester City. Shilton told Leicester, 'Either he goes or I go', and I think Paul Robinson may say the same to Leeds. You have to believe in yourself as a goalkeeper.

"When Nicky Weaver played for Manchester City against Arsenal at Highbury last season, I was very impressed. He's had problems since and needs to rebuild his confidence, but he has talent too."

THE FUTURE

"The pressure on David Seaman is immense, because critics are just waiting for him to make a mistake. It has happened to so many England goalkeepers when they have got to a certain age. People don't understand that goalkeepers always make mistakes – the best ones just make fewer.

"It must be remembered that being a goalkeeper in the Premiership is totally different to being an international goalkeeper. That's partly down to style of games, but it's basically down to the pressure of being the national team's number one.

"I'm hugely impressed with all the guys I've mentioned. If England qualify, the player who wears the jersey in Japan will be the one who is the most consistent, makes least mistakes and, most important of all, makes the right decisions."

ENGLAND'S

SEAMAN

1

NUMBER...

Clockwise: Paul Robinson, Nigel Martyn, David James , Nicky Weaver and Richard Wright all have prospects, but David Seaman has the experience.

THE FA CUP

ROUND 3

There had already been some shocks by the time Premiership and First Division teams entered the fray in the third round. Dagenham & Redbridge were among four non-league sides to make it to this stage and they faced the daunting task of taking on Charlton Athletic at the Valley. Amazingly, a team which cost a total of £5,000 to assemble outplayed their Premiership opponents and were unlucky not to go through. Dagenham took the lead just before half-time when a firm header by Junior McDougald finished a typically fluent move, but a deflected shot by John Salako in the 86th minutes saved Charlton's blushes.

"They were the better side," admitted Addicks boss, Alan Curbishley, afterwards.

The replay at Victoria Road was equally tense, but a Shaun Newton goal in the first minute of extra-time finally killed off Dagenham's hopes.

Another Conference side, Kingstonian, sprung a surprise away to Third Division team Southend, winning 1–0 with a goal by Eddie Akuamoah. On the surface, it was an extraordinary result for a side languishing in 20th position in the Conference, but 55-year-old Kingstonian boss Geoff Chapple is known for his giant-killing exploits as manager of non-league teams. The victory took his total of league victims in FA Cup matches to seven.

Yeovil Town who'd beaten Blackpool in the previous round, put up a good fight against Bolton at the Reebok Stadium but went down to a 1–2 defeat. The other non-league team, Morecambe, who boast

Fabien Barthez couldn't fool Di Canio!

Eddie Akuamoah celebrates his winning goal for non-league Kingstonian against Southend United.

The FA Cup, the most famous club cup competition in the world came back to life in 2001. Giant-killing acts, penalty shoot-outs, miraculous comebacks... the tournament had it all. Let's re-live the highlights...

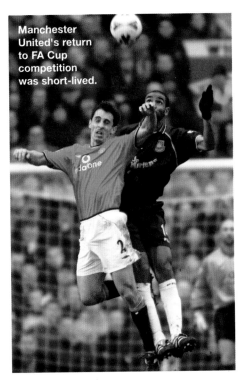

Manchester United's return to FA Cup competition was short-lived.

Jim "Bullseye" Bowen as a celebrity fan, got a 3–0 thumping at home to Ipswich Town.

Meanwhile FA Cup holders, Chelsea, eased through to the next round beating Peterbrough 5–0 at Stamford Bridge. Leeds and Arsenal crept through by 1–0 margins against Barnsley and Carlisle United respectively and Liverpool crushed Rotherham United 3–0 at Anfield. Manchester United, back in the FA Cup after a one-year hiatus, also progressed beating First Division pace-setters Fulham 2–1 at Craven Cottage thanks to a brilliant 89th-minute winner by Teddy Sheringham.

ROUND 4

West Ham United caused the shock of the round beating Manchester United 1–0. Having lost on 11 successive visits to Old Trafford, the Hammers were given little chance by pundits, but Italian maverick Paolo Di Canio's 75th-minute goal knocked out the Premiership champs. A perceptive through ball by Frederic Kanoute put Di Canio through and he ignored goalkeeper Fabien Barthez's bizarre attempt to put him off (Barthez raised his arm to claim offside) to cooly slot the ball into the net. It was Manchester United's first defeat in the FA Cup since they lost at Barnsley in a fifth round replay in 1998.

Arsenal had no such trouble demolishing London neighbours Queens Park Rangers by a 6–0 margin at Loftus Road. And in a battle of Premiership giants, Liverpool prevailed 2–0 against Leeds United at Elland Road. Robbie Fowler, who was rumoured to be leaving Liverpool, produced a brilliant all-round performance and when his shot ricocheted back off the post in the 87th minute, Nicky Barmby was on hand to give the visitors the lead. A rocket shot by Emile Heskey just before the final whistle made sure of victory.

Elsewhere, First Division strugglers Tranmere Rovers stunned Everton in a Merseyside derby winning 3–0. Tottenham fans' belief that they always win the cup in a year ending with a "1" grew stronger as they came back from 2–0 down against Charlton at the Valley to record a 4–2 victory. Three second-half goals in five minutes – a Richard Rufus own goal, a free-kick by Darren Anderton and a run and shot by Oyvind Leonhardsen – turned the game for George Graham's side and Sergei Rebrov's 82nd-minute goal clinched the win.

After a 1–1 draw at the Riverside stadium, Wimbledon beat Middlesbrough 3–1 in the replay at Selhurst Park to set up an intriguing tie against Wycombe Wanders managed by former Crazy

The Chairboys go wild!

THE ROAD TO CARDIFF

ROUND 3

Newcastle United 1	Aston Villa 1
replay: Aston Villa 1	*Newcastle United 0*
Blackburn Rovers 2	Chester City 0
Morecambe 0	Ipswich Town 3
Leeds United 1	Barnsley 0
Derby County 3	West Bromwich Albion 2
Watford 1	Everton 2
Carlisle United 0	Arsenal 1
Walsall 2	West Ham United 3
Swindon Town 0	Coventry City 2
Bolton Wanderers 2	Yeovil Town 1
Southend United 0	Kingstonian 1
Huddersfield Town 0	Bristol City 2
Leicester City 3	York City 0
Charlton Athletic 1	Dagenham & Redbridge 1
replay: Dagenham & R. 0 Charlton Athletic 1	
AFC Bournemouth 2	Gillingham 3
Chelsea 5	Peterborough United 0
Wimbledon 2	Notts County 2
replay: Notts County 0 Wimbledon 1	
Leyton Orient 0	Tottenham Hotspur 1
Burnley 2	Scunthorpe United 2
replay: Scunthorpe 1 Burnley 1 – Scunthorpe win 5–4 on pens	
Preston North End 0	Stockport County 1
Manchester City 3	Birmingham City 2
Portsmouth 1	Tranmere Rovers 2
Bradford City 0	Middlesbrough 1
Sunderland 0	Crystal Palace 0
replay: Crystal Palace 2 Sunderland 4	
Cardiff City 1	Crewe Alexandra 1
replay: Crewe Alexandra 2 Cardiff City 1	
Southampton 1	Sheffield United 0
Fulham 1	Manchester United 2
Liverpool 3	Rotherham United 0
Wycombe Wanderers 1	Grimsby Town 1
replay: Grimsby Town 1 Wycombe Wanderers 3	
Nottingham Forest 0	Wolverhampton Wanderers 1
Luton Town 3	Queens Park Rangers 3
replay: Queens Park Rangers 2 Luton Town 1	
Sheffield Wednesday2	Norwich City 1

ROUND 4

Sunderland 1	Ipswich Town 0
Gillingham 2	Chelsea 4
Middlesbrough 0	Wimbledon 0
replay: Wimbledon 3 Middlesbrough 1	
Bristol City 1	Kingstonian 1
replay: Kingstonian 0 Bristol City 1	
Bolton Wanderers 5	Scunthorpe United 1
Blackburn Rovers 0	Derby County 0
replay: Derby County 2 Blackburn Rovers 5	
Manchester City 1	Coventry City 0
Crewe Alexandra 0	Stockport County 1
Southampton 3	Sheffield Wednesday 1
Wycombe Wanderers 2	Wolverhampton Wanderers 1
Charlton Athletic 2	Tottenham Hotspur 4
Leeds United 0	Liverpool 2
Manchester United 0	West Ham United 1
Everton 0	Tranmere Rovers 3
QPR 0	Arsenal 6
Aston Villa 1	Leicester City 3

Gang member, Lawrie Sanchez. Sanchez's team beat Wolves 2–1. Sam Parkin, 19 years-old and on loan from Chelsea, came on as sub and headed home the Chairboys' 83rd-minute winner.

Geoff Chapple's plucky Kingstonian team were on the verge of beating Second Division Bristol City and making the fifth round draw. Carpet cleaner Phil Wingfield had given Kingstonian the lead on 57 minutes and their supporters were ready to celebrate as the final whistle approached. But then, cruelly, City's top-scorer, Tony Thorpe, stabbed in an injury-time equaliser with the last kick of the game. The replay was equally competitive and it took an 88th-minute goal by Bristol City's Scott Murray to finally kill of Kingstonian. Boss Chapple was gracious in defeat saying: "The better side won, but I'm proud of my boys. It's been a fairytale story for us."

ROUND 5

Wycombe boss, Lawrie Sanchez, was delighted to beat Wimbledon, the team he scored an FA Cup winning goal for in 1998. The Chairboys came back from 2–0 down to tie the first game 2–2 and the score was also deadlocked at 2–2 after extra-time in the replay. Wycombe finally triumphed 8–7 on penalties when Mark Williams of Wimbledon missed the 20th spot-kick!

Cup holders Chelsea's trophy reign was ended by Arsenal at Highbury. Two late goals by substitute Sylvain Wiltord secured a 3–1 win but the amazing thing was that no-one was sent-off. "They needed to put on boxing gloves," smiled defeated Chelsea coach Claudio Ranieri afterwards.

Tranmere's giant-killing exploits continued as they beat Southampton 4–3 at Prenton Park. Glenn Hoddle's team were 3–0 up at half-time, but Rovers' striker Paul Rideout bagged a 21-minute hat-trick to level the scores before Stuart Barlow scrambled the winner to stun the Saints.

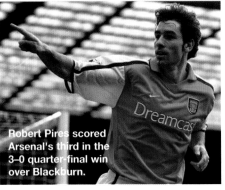

Robert Pires scored Arsenal's third in the 3–0 quarter-final win over Blackburn.

Elsewhere, West Ham continued their good run of away form in the cup by beating Sunderland 1–0 at the Stadium of Light and Liverpool dispatched Manchester City 4–2 at Maine Road. Oh, and Spurs kept the George Graham bandwagon rolling with a 4–0 demolition of Stockport…

QUARTER-FINAL

Unbelievable… that was the only word to describe Second Division Wycombe Wanderers 2–1 FA Cup quarter-final win over Leicester City at Filbert Street. With six centre-forwards injured before the match, Wycombe boss Lawrie Sanchez put a "Strikers wanted" notice on Ceefax. Unknown Belfast-born Ghanain Roy Essandoh answered the call. He was given a two-week contract and a place on the subs bench for the big match.

It was a tense game and when Wycombe were denied a clear penalty with the score at 1–1, the normally placid Lawrie Sanchez exploded with rage. The referee sent him off and Sanchez was forced to watch the rest of the game on a TV monitor. He was busy pacing the floor in the 90th minute when a looping cross was headed across goal by Jamie Bates and

powered in by… guess who? Cyber striker Roy Essandoh, of course! At the end of the game there were tears of joy for Wycombe staff, players and fans as they hailed an historic victory.

In the other quarter-finals, Liverpool proved too strong for Mersey neighbours Tranmere, managed by ex-Red John Aldridge. First-half strikes by Danny Murphy and Michael Owen gave Gerard Houllier's men breathing space. Although Rovers did manage to narrow the gap to 3–2 on the hour mark, a late Fowler penalty earned Pool a semi-final tie against Wycombe.

The Arsenal–Blackburn tie was effectively over within 35 minutes. Sylvain Wiltord (2 mins), Tony Adams (5 mins) and Robert Pires (35 mins) all got on the scoresheet as the Gunners blasted out the First Division high-fliers.

In the London derby, Tottenham squeezed past West Ham in a 3–2 thriller at Upton Park. Gary Doherty was the hero scoring a 62nd-minute winner prompting fears for Paolo Di Canio's health. The enigmatic Italian had previously said he'd kill himself if he didn't win a trophy with West Ham!

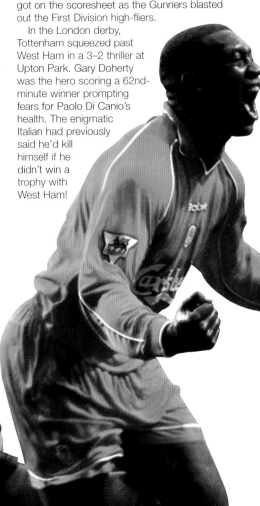

Veteran striker Paul Rideout was the hat-trick hero for Tranmere Rovers in their thrilling 4–3 comeback win over Southampton in round five.

Heskey's goal helped to kill off Wycombe's plucky challenge.

Dejection for the Gunners, another trophy for Owen and co.

SEMI-FINAL

And then there were four...

The Liverpool-Wycombe semi-final was played at Villa Park with half the capacity 40,000 crowd made up of happy Chairboys fans. Wycombe again put up a brilliant display despite an obvious gap in class between the two sides. Dogged defensive work, and a marvellous performance by their goalkeeper Martin Taylor (a former coalminer), kept the score goalless until the 78th minute when substitute Emile Heskey headed home. A delicious curled free-kick by Robbie Fowler five minutes later put the result beyond doubt, but Wycombe never stopped battling and were rewarded with a consolation goal by captain Keith Ryan. It was the end of a fairytale run which had restored the magic to the FA Cup once more.

At Old Trafford, Spurs' dreams of a date with destiny were shattered as fierce rivals Arsenal beat them 2–1. Spurs prospects weren't helped by the sacking of George Graham and new manager Glenn Hoddle had just a week to prepare his new team. Despite taking an early lead through Garry Doherty, Spurs were ultimately outplayed by Arsenal and goals from

Patrick Vieira and Robert Pires earned the Gunners a Cup final meeting with Liverpool.

THE FINAL

The 2001 FA Cup final will be remembered as Michael Owen's match after his two fantastic late goals gave Liverpool a 2–1 victory at the Millennium Stadium in Cardiff.

Until Owen struck in the 83rd and 88th minutes, it was hard to imagine Liverpool would score at all, let alone win, such had been Arsenal's dominance. The key moment of the match occurred in the 17th minute when Thierry Henry's goal-bound shot was handled by Liverpool defender Stephane Henchoz. If the ref had seen the offence, it would have been an Arsenal penalty and a red card for Henchoz.

The Gunners did finally break through in the 72nd minute when Freddie Ljungberg scored, but the genius of Michael Owen foiled them. First, Owen drilled a loose ball into the bottom corner, then five minutes later he latched on to a hopeful long ball by Patrik Berger and powered an angled left-foot drive past David Seaman.

It was a fittingly astonishing end to an extraordinary competition.

ROUND 5

Leicester City 3	Bristol City 0
Wycombe Wanderers 2	Wimbledon 2
replay: Wimbledon 2 Wycombe Wanderers 2 – Wycombe won 8–7 on pens	
Bolton Wanderers 1	Blackburn Rovers 1
replay: Blackburn Rovers 3 Bolton Wanderers 0	
Tottenham Hotspur 4	Stockport County 0
Liverpool 4	Manchester City 2
Arsenal 3	Chelsea 1
Southampton 0	Tranmere Rovers 0
replay: Tranmere 4 Southampton 3	
Sunderland 0	West Ham United 1

QUARTER-FINAL

Tranmere Rovers 2	Liverpool 4
Leicester City 1	Wycombe Wanderers 2
West Ham United 2	Tottenham Hotspur 3
Arsenal 3	Blackburn Rovers 0

SEMI-FINAL

Tottenham Hotspur 1	Arsenal 2
Wycombe Wanderers 1	Liverpool 2

FINAL

Arsenal 1	Liverpool 2

ENGLAND EXPECTS!

What happens when England's top stars get together for training? Check out these insider pics and find out...

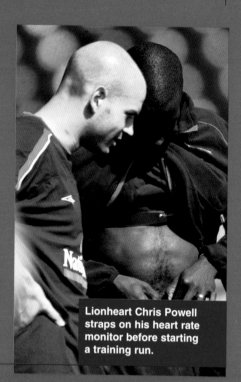

Lionheart Chris Powell straps on his heart rate monitor before starting a training run.

Teddy adjusts his equipment after getting his pulse checked by coach Sammy Lee.

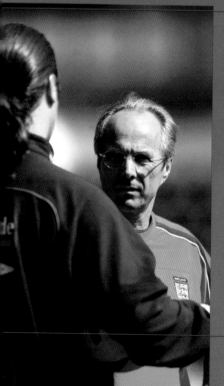

'What is it about England players and haircuts these days?' Coach Sven Goran Eriksson ponders ponytails and mohicans in the summer sun!

"A word in your ear, son." Alan Smith takes a little advice before heading practice begins.

Gareth and Teddy feel the burn...

m triangle.

Top Gunner Martin Keown has a bit of a giggle.

Rio executes his famous bum trap skill and big Emile puts the squeeze on captain Becks!

Even super-fit Steven Gerrard is worn out by the end of the session!

Since the Premier League was formed in 1992, Manchester United have won the title seven times in nine attempts. In 2001/02, the Old Trafford giants will be aiming to win their fourth title in a row. Can anyone put the skids under Sir Fergie's Red juggernaut?

F ollowing their exit at the quarter-final stage of the Champions League to Bayern Munich in April, disappointed Manchester United captain Roy Keane voiced his opinion that, "Maybe the success is coming to an end."

At domestic level at least, such talk seems premature. In 1999/2000, United romped to title glory, winning by a record 18-point margin and scoring 97 goals (another record) in the process. Last year, the Reds' dominance was such that they pretty much had the title neatly wrapped up with a bow on top by Christmas. Hardly the sign of a club in decline!

And the frightening thing for the contenders to United's crown is that most of the Reds' key players are either approaching or are in their peak years. Stars like Roy Keane (30), Paul Scholes (26), Ole Gunnar Solskjaer (28), Jaap Stam (29), Andy Cole (29), Ryan Giggs (27), David Beckham (26) are hardly ready to be pensioned off yet! And when you also consider United's talented, young, homegrown players such as classy defender Wes Brown and wing skillster Luke Chadwick plus big-money summer signings like £19 million man Ruud Van Nistelrooy, it's clear that Manchester United are still very much the team to beat in English football.

There appear to be only three teams with realistic prospects of mounting a sustained challenge to Manchester United – Liverpool, Arsenal and Leeds United.

Liverpool will be buoyant after their cup treble success, and they now appear to have strength in depth comparable to United. For all their quality players though, a lot may

depend on young Steven Gerrard. Gerrard adds bite to a Liverpool team that has sometimes lacked competitiveness in the past and the midfield maestro could play a key role in improving Liverpool's dodgy away league form. By the time Manchester United had mathematically clinched the 2000/01 Premiership title back in April, they had lost just two matches on the road, whereas Houllier's men had lost seven. Liverpool will have to start winning matches in Leicester and Middlesbrough if they want to put the pressure on United this time around.

"With Liverpool, it's the old thing – they've got to get the consistency," notes Manchester United winger Ryan Giggs. "They showed a bit of that towards the end of last season so we'll just have to see whether they can make the next step forward or not."

Arsenal, meanwhile, will be desperate to get back on the trophy rostrum after three silverware-free seasons. Like Liverpool, they have a high-quality squad, but their pitiful away form cost them dearly in 2000/01. Arsene Wenger also has the

worry of ageing players in key positions. For instance, Tony Adams has been the bedrock of the Gunners' defence and an inspiration to the whole team for over a decade, but the old warhorse is now nearing retirement. If Wenger can't find adequate cover for Adams, it could be another season of frustration down at Highbury.

Old age is not a problem for David O'Leary's team at Leeds. Although, O'Leary has said in the past that Manchester United are unstoppable and his realistic aim is to finish second in the Premiership, he has a wonderful young team for whom the sky is the limit. Last season,

UNITED?

Leeds finished fourth in the table despite being crippled by injuries. Stars like Harry Kewell and David Batty were all on the casualty list for long periods, but their absence had the positive effect of allowing O'Leary's younger players valuable first-team experience. Without the distraction of the Champions League, the Yorkshire club could make a serious challenge for the league championship title they last won in 1992.

For the rest of the teams in the Premiership, the future is less predictable. Chelsea were supposed to be title challengers last year, but not for the first time the Blues lack of consistency let them down. The surprise sacking of Gianluca Vialli and subsequent replacement of the Italian with Claudio Ranieri doesn't appear to have improved matters so far either. Ranieri's strange policy of only speaking to the media when his team loses is just one of the symptoms of a club in transition. Strange times indeed at Stamford Bridge!

Elsewhere, many neutrals will be hoping that Manager of the Year George Burley can continue to drive Ipswich Town forward following their marvellous 2000/01 campaign. Meanwhile, fans of perennial mid-table clubs like Tottenham, Aston Villa and Middlesbrough will be hoping to step up towards a top six-finish. And after their close shaves with relegation last season, Derby County and Everton will be trying to keep away from the drop zone this time. But as promoted clubs Fulham, Blackburn Rovers and Bolton Wanderers have the financial clout to survive in the Premiership, May 2002 could see some well-established teams take the plunge into the Division One.

Whatever the final outcome, it's shaping up to be the most exciting Premiership season for many years. So get involved, put on your team scarf and, win or lose, make sure you sing yer hearts out for the lads!

STYLE FILE

What was Gazza thinking? Nothing, probably... Eric on the other hand is always full of deep thoughts (Like, Qui mange all the pies?!).

Emanuel and Marc look just dandy in their suits. But, Macca, oh dear... that bow tie is surely criminal.

David Seaman. So much we could say, so little time... Will he per-lease LOSE THAT PONYTAIL??!!! In comparison, Steffen's jumper seems quite acceptable.

David James in the worst FA Cup final suit ever. Mind you, wonder what the Dons wore for their trip to Wembley – tracksuits?

Talking of pies, Santa Redknapp look lies he's had more than his fair share of the mince pies and sherry.

MAGIC MOMENTS

No 3: Andy Townsend

" I've chosen Thierry Henry's incredible goal against Manchester United at Highbury last October. It was just a moment of pure class from a world-class striker. He received the ball with his back to goal on the edge of the penalty box and United defenders all around him. In the blink of an eye, he managed to flick the ball up, turn and hit a fabulous dipping volley. The fact that he managed to beat Fabien Barthez, who I consider to be the best goalkeeper in the world, from that range tells you everything about the quality of the strike. **"**

STAT ATTACK!

The top shot-stoppers, the fastest goalscorers, the most accurate passers, the dirtiest players… every statistic on the 2000/01 Premiership you didn't even realise you needed to know is right here!

THE TOP GOALSCORERS

PLAYER	GOALS	% SHOTS SCORED
Jimmy Floyd Hasselbaink	23	20.4%
Marcus Stewart	19	23.5%
Mark Viduka	17	26.6%
Thierry Henry	17	13.8%
Michael Owen	16	22.9%
Teddy Sheringham	15	26.8%
Emile Heskey	14	17.1%
Kevin Phillips	14	12.5%
Alen Boksic	12	18.2%
Alan Smith	11	18.6%

THE FASTEST GOALS

PLAYER	MATCH	TIME
1 Ledley King	Bradford v TOTTENHAM	10 secs
2 Mark Viduka	LEEDS v Charlton	12 secs
3 Craig Bellamy	Leicester v COVENTRY	45 secs
4 Dion Dublin	ASTON VILLA v Everton	1 min 11 secs
5 David Beckham	Man City v MAN UNITED	1 min 36 secs

PASS MASTERS

PLAYER	PASSES	ACCURACY
1 Roy Keane	2,184	86.7%
2 Jim Magilton	2,122	80.2%
3 Paul Merson	2,085	72.6%
4 David Beckham	2,081	77.1%
5 Gary Speed	1,815	72.3%

TOP TACKLERS

PLAYER	TACKLES	% TACKLES WON
1 Olivier Dacourt	173	71.1%
2 Stuart McCall	148	61.5%
3 Michael Carrick	143	66.4%
4 Nigel Winterburn	131	68.7%
5 Steven Gerrard	128	68.8%

THEY LIKE TO DRIBBLE

PLAYER	DRIBBLES	COMPLETION RATE
1 Frederic Kanoute	145	38.6%
2 Ryan Giggs	144	44.4%
3 Thierry Henry	129	34.1%
4 Mark Viduka	125	29.6%
5 Paolo Di Canio	117	42.7%

SUPER SAVERS

PLAYER	SAVES	% SHOTS SAVED
Neil Sullivan	142	73.6%
Mart Poom	140	71.1%
Sander Westerveld	122	75.8%
Mark Schwarzer	117	77.5%
Paul Jones	117	73.1%

THE DIRTY DOZEN

PLAYER	FOULS	YELLOW CARDS	RED CARDS
1 Olivier Dacourt	94	13	0
2 Ashley Ward	95	9	0
3 Don Hutchison	80	11	1
4 Alan Smith	90	7	1
5 Paolo Wanchope	85	9	0
6 Deon Burton	88	4	1
7 Gary Speed	74	8	1
8 George Boateng	74	9	0
9 Niall Quinn	85	5	0
10 Thomas Gravesen	69	7	1
11 Dion Dublin	90	2	0
12 Patrick Vieira	67	5	2

THE ALL-ROUNDERS

PLAYER	CLUB	OPTA INDEX SCORE*
1 Fabien Barthez	Manchester United	990
2 Tim Flowers	Leicester City	983
3 Neil Sullivan	Tottenham	974
4 Mark Schwarzer	Middlesbrough	892
5 Mart Poom	Derby County	890

BEST DEFENDERS

PLAYER	CLUB	OPTA INDEX SCORE*
1 Sami Hyppia	Liverpool	1086
2 Ian Harte	Leeds United	1046
3 Tony Adams	Arsenal	1046
4 Marcel Desailly	Chelsea	1039
5 John Terry	Chelsea	1037

BEST MIDFIELDERS

PLAYER	CLUB	OPTA INDEX SCORE*
1 Roy Keane	Manchester United	1377
2 Patrick Vieira	Arsenal	1088
3 Steven Gerrard	Liverpool	1034
4 Mark Kinsella	Charlton	999
5 Nicky Butt	Manchester United	980

BEST ATTACKING MIDFIELDERS

PLAYER	CLUB	OPTA INDEX SCORE*
1 David Beckham	Manchester United	1347
2 Paul Scholes	Manchester United	1088
3 Robert Pires	Arsenal	1060
4 Freddie Ljungberg	Arsenal	1056
5 Gustavo Poyet	Chelsea	1052

BEST STRIKERS

PLAYER	CLUB	OPTA INDEX SCORE*
1 Michael Owen	Liverpool	1083
2 Teddy Sheringham	Manchester United	1057
3 Thierry Henry	Arsenal	1025
4 Marcus Stewart	Ipswich	1001
5 Jimmy Floyd Hasselbaink	Chelsea	984

opta.co.uk

* How the Opta Scoring System works… A team of specially-trained Opta analysts monitor and record every touch of the ball in the FA Carling Premiership using state-of-the-art digital software. Each touch is awarded plus or minus points based on a system originally devised in conjunction with former England coach Don Howe. The Opta database then averages out each player's marks over the course of the season to produce the Index scores, which gives an excellent guide to the player's form.

THE SEASON IN NUMBERS

0	Southampton were the only side not to be awarded a penalty.
2	Michael Carrick's goals-to-shots percentage, the lowest ratio of any player to have scored a goal.
5	The number of times David Ginola played the full 90 minutes for Aston Villa in the Premiership.
6	Headed goals by Mark Viduka, the most by any Premiership player.
8	Most goals in a single Premiership game (Arsenal 5 Charlton 3).
9	Penalties awarded at Goodison Park, more than at any other Premiership ground.
14	Hat-tricks in the 2000/01 Premiership.
17	Clean sheets for Arsenal and Manchester United, the most in the Premiership.
19	The number of times Manchester United hit the woodwork, the most in the Premiership.
20	The number of Premiership games without a booking this season.
21	Overseas players used by Chelsea in the 2000/01 Premiership campaign.
27	The average age of a Premiership player in 2000/01.
28	0-0 draws in the Premiership.
31	Own goals scored in the Premiership.
33	Yellow cards for Ipswich, the fewest in the Premiership.
34	Players used by West Ham in the Premiership, no other team used as many.
38	Southampton's Wayne Bridge was the only outfield player to have played the full 90 minutes in all 38 Premiership games.
39	Ian Harte's shooting accuracy, percentage-wise, from free-kicks.
45	The percentage of all Premiership goals that were scored in the first half.
47	The percentage of Jimmy Floyd Hasselbaink's shots from outside the area that hit the target.
51	Dion Dublin had more headed goal attempts than any other Premiership player.
53	Shots off target by Moustapha Hadji. No other midfielder fired in as many wayward efforts at goal.
55	The number of times free-kicks were moved ten yards closer to goal because of dissent.
62	The percentage of players used in the Premiership who were born in the UK.
63	The number of games Liverpool played in all competitions.
64	Red cards in the Premiership.
75	The number of times Thierry Henry was caught offside, the most in the Premiership.
76	Percentage of Roy Keane's passes in the final third of the pitch which found a team-mate, the best ratio in the Premiership.
81	Yellow cards for Derby County, more than any other Premiership team.
83	Percentage of Arsenal's Premiership goals scored by overseas players.
89	The number of times Frederic Kanoute was dispossessed when dribbling with the ball, more than any other Premiership player.
91	David James' catch success rate (%) for Aston Villa.
93	The percentage of Juan Pablo Angel's shots which didn't result in a goal.
96	Shots on target from outside the area by Manchester United, the most in the Premiership.
100	Paul Boertien and Paolo Vernazza were the only two players to have a 100 percent goals-to-shots ratio. Both scored from their only shot of the season.

FANTASY PREMIERSHIP XI

If you could have your pick of the Premiership's finest talent, who would get in your first team? Here, ITV pundits Barry Venison and Andy Townsend turn fantasy football managers to choose their all-star XIs. To be fair, they've sorted out a couple of decent sides!

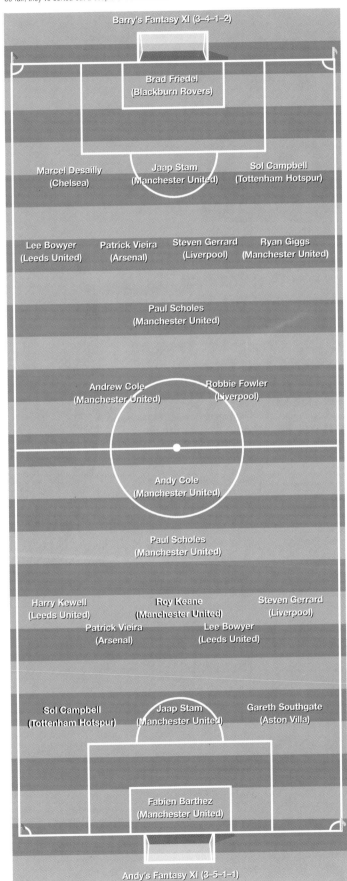

Barry's Fantasy XI (3–4–1–2)

Brad Friedel
(Blackburn Rovers)

Marcel Desailly
(Chelsea)

Jaap Stam
(Manchester United)

Sol Campbell
(Tottenham Hotspur)

Lee Bowyer
(Leeds United)

Patrick Vieira
(Arsenal)

Steven Gerrard
(Liverpool)

Ryan Giggs
(Manchester United)

Paul Scholes
(Manchester United)

Andrew Cole
(Manchester United)

Robbie Fowler
(Liverpool)

Andy Cole
(Manchester United)

Paul Scholes
(Manchester United)

Harry Kewell
(Leeds United)

Roy Keane
(Manchester United)

Steven Gerrard
(Liverpool)

Patrick Vieira
(Arsenal)

Lee Bowyer
(Leeds United)

Sol Campbell
(Tottenham Hotspur)

Jaap Stam
(Manchester United)

Gareth Southgate
(Aston Villa)

Fabien Barthez
(Manchester United)

Andy's Fantasy XI (3–5–1–1)

"Opposing strikers wouldn't get much change out of Desailly, Stam and Campbell... even if they manage to get past Vieira and Gerrard, which is unlikely! I've had to choose five midfielders because there's so many good ones about and this little lot should provide plenty of ammo for Andy Cole and Robbie Fowler up front."

"Like Baz, I can't ignore the quality of midfielders in the Premiership now – that's why I'm playing a slightly different formation so I can have six in the side! I'm taking advantage of Gerrard's versatility to play him on the right and Harry Kewell just gets my vote over Ryan Giggs on the left."

WORLD CUP 2002

Next summer sees another festival of international football with the biggest, the brightest and the best tournament in sport – the World Cup finals. We take a sneak peek to see what's in store.

On May 31 next year, 32 teams will battle it out in Japan and Korea for football's ultimate prize. France will be there as the current holders. Will England? That depends on how results have gone in the qualifying stages. But what can teams who make it expect to find?

THE VENUE

The 2002 World Cup will kick off in Korea on May 31 and conclude four weeks later on June 30 in Japan. Matches will be played in 20 host cities, ten in Japan and ten in Korea. The Japanese cities are: Sapporo, Nigata, Miyagi, Saitama, Ibaraki, Kobe, Yokohama, Shizuoka, Osaka and Oita. The Korean cities are: Seoul, Incheon, Suwon, Daejeon, Jeonju, Gwangju, Daegu, Ulsan, Busan and Seogwipo.

THE FOOTBALL CULTURE

It used to be that baseball was the most popular game in Japan but no longer. The emergence of the J.League, Japan's professional league, has meant that football has never been more popular. Of course, Japan have added a few touches of its own. A number of the players are more like pop stars with trendy brightly dyed hair or goatee beards and teenage girls shriek and scream if they get injured. There are samba bands at some grounds and gaudy mascots. There has also been an influx of established players over the years, such as England striker Gary Lineker at Grampus Eight, Brazil's Zico at Kashima and Germany's Pierre Littbarski at JEF United.

Since the J.League took off, you can buy J.League crisps, J.League face paint, even J.League curry! "J. League" was rather bizarrely voted "Word of the Year" in a national newspaper.

THE TEAMS

A record 198 football associations took part in the initial qualifying procedures. Of those 32 will compete in the finals. France, Japan and Korea automatically qualify. By November 2001, the other 29 teams should all be known. It's the most democratic competition in the world. Teams of all standards can enter, such as American Samoa, who were crushed 31–0 by Australia in qualifying.

THE DRAW

After all 32 teams are known, a draw will take place on December 1 in the city of Busan in Korea. The format is the same as in France '98. There will be eight groups of four teams in the first round. Each team in the group plays the other three in a league format. The top two teams from each group advance to the second round stage which is knockout. Quarter- and semi-finals follow before the final in Yokohama on June 30.

TELEVISION

All matches will be shown on terrestrial television. This is because the entire tournament is classed as a "listed event", i.e. you don't have to pay to watch it.

Can France retain their crown ?

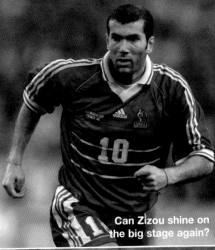

Can Zizou shine on the big stage again?

Ronaldo could rebuild his reputation at World Cup 2002.

Steven Gerrard has a chance to become a world star.

Nakata will be the most popular player with home fans.

who made his name in Italy's Serie A. Meanwhile Brazil's Ronaldo will be desperate to prove himself on the biggest stage after the injury setbacks of the last few years. And Zinedine Zidane will be crucial if France are to maintain their dominance of world football. If England make it to the finals, Michael Owen, David Beckham and Steven Gerrard are just three of the players who have a chance to write themselves into the history books.

THE PLAYERS

The tournament is sure to throw up some new stars, but a few faces will already be familiar to the watching millions. For home fans, the biggest draw is undoubtedly Hidetoshi Nakata, the Japanese star

THE FINAL

The final will be played at the 70,564-seat International Stadium Yokohama, which is the biggest stadium in the country. It is the home of the J. League team the Yokohama F. Marinos.

N1405

OMENTS

No 4: Des Lynam

"

Manchester United's 6–1 demolition of Arsenal in March finally killed off the 2000/01 Premiership race and emphasised to me their superiority.

After months of watching from the subs bench while Teddy Sheringham and Andy Cole banged in the goals, Dwight Yorke came in and destroyed Arsene Wenger's side in the space of 22 minutes with a brilliant hat-trick. That's the strength in depth of United – Yorke was top scorer in the Reds Treble season, but no-one can rest on their laurels at Old Trafford.

"

GO GLOBAL

Football is an international language or so they say, so why not test your knowledge of the global game?

UP FOR THE CUP!
Name the competition and the current holder of the trophy!

1 **2** **3** **4**

MAKE THE CONNECTION...
Which top European club connects these two former England managers?

INTERNATIONAL QUIZ
1 Ryan Giggs played international schoolboy football for which country?
2 Which country has won the World Cup the most times?
3 How old was Michael Owen when he played in his first World Cup finals in 1998?
4 What nationality is Sunderland goalkeeper Thomas Sorensen?
5 Name two of the three Spanish teams that reached the quarter-finals of the 2000/01 Champions League?
6 Which Brazilian superstar was voted the 1999 European Footballer of the Year?
7 Who did France beat in the 1998 World Cup final?
8 Which two teams share the Olympic Stadium in Rome?
9 How old was legendary winger Stanley Matthews when he won his last England cap: a) 37 b) 42 or c) 47?
10 Name the coach of the Bayern Munich team that won the 2001 Champions League?
11 Which Italian club does Zinedine Zidane play for?
12 Which Parma and Cameroon player was voted the 2000 African Footballer of the Year?
13 Former England winger Chris Waddle played for the only French club ever to win the European Cup – was it a) Olympique Marseille b) Paris St. Germain or c) Auxerre
14 David Beckham was sent off during the 1998 World Cup finals for fouling which Argentinian player?
15 Zinedine Zidane was voted the FIFA World Player of the Year 2000 beating which Portugese player into second place?
16 Which Liverpool hotshot scored 32 goals in the 1983/84 season and won the European Golden Boot?
17 Newcastle's Nolberto Solano is an international for which country?
18 How old was Patrick Kluivert when he scored the winning goal for Ajax against AC Milan in the 1995 European Cup Final?
19 Who was the coach of the French team that triumphed in Euro 2000?
20 Which international team does Derby County captain Darryl Powell play for?

STADIUM SPECTACULAR
Can you put a name to these famous European stadiums.
1. Stade De France, Paris 2. Old Trafford, England 3. Nou Camp, Barcelona 4. San Siro, Italy

A **B** **C** **D**

SPOT THE STAR!
Can you identify these world superstars!

1 2 3 4 5 6

INTERNATIONAL QUIZ 1. England 2. Brazil (four times) 3. Michael Owen 4. Danish 5. Valencia, Real Madrid and/or Deportivo La Coruna 6. Rivaldo 7. France 8. AS Roma and Lazio 9 c) 47 10. Ottmar Hitzfeld 11. Juventus 12. Patrick Mboma 13. a) Olympique Marseille 14. Diego Simeone 15. Luis Figo 16. Ian Rush 17. Peru 18. 18 19. Roger Lemerre 20. Jamaica UP FOR THE CUP! 1. World Cup – France 2. UEFA Cup – Liverpool 3. European Cup – Bayern Munich 4. European Championship – France SPOT THE STAR! 1. Alessandro Del Piero 2. Oliver Kahn 3. Luis Figo 4. Edwin Van Der Sar 5. Roy Keane 6. Tore Andre Flo MAKE THE CONNECTION Barcelona – they were both manager there STADIUM SPECTACULAR 1. C 2. A 3. D, 4. B